# NEEDS ASSESSMENT

# SAGE HUMAN SERVICES GUIDES, VOLUME 14

# SAGE HUMAN SERVICES GUIDES

*a series of books edited by ARMAND LAUFFER and published in cooperation with the University of Michigan School of Social Work.*

A **SAGE** HUMAN SERVICES GUIDE  **14**

# NEEDS ASSESSMENT
## A Model for Community Planning

## Keith A. NEUBER
William T. ATKINS, James A. JACOBSON,
and Nicholas A. REUTERMAN

*Published in cooperation with the*
*University of Michigan School of Social Work*

**SAGE** PUBLICATIONS    Beverly Hills    London

*For information address:*

SAGE Publications, Inc.
275 South Beverly Drive
Beverly Hills, California 90212

SAGE Publications Ltd
28 Banner Street
London EC1Y 8QE, England

Printed in the United States of America

**Library of Congress Cataloging in Publication Data**
Main entry under title:

Needs assessment

   (Sage human services guides ; v. 14)
   Bibliography: p.
   1. Social services—Planning—Mathematical models—Handbooks, manuals, etc. I. Neuber, Keith A.
HV40.N43    361.2'5    79-27929
ISBN 0-8039-1396-6

SIXTH PRINTING, 1985

# C O N T E N T S

# ABOUT THIS BOOK

Almost all social agencies and community groups have at some time faced the need to assess needs. For many, the task has seemed insurmountable because of cost or lack of available technical expertise. CONA—the community-oriented needs assessment model presented in this guide—should prove a welcome addition to the *Sage Human Service Guides*. It gives step by step directions for conducting presurvey activities, setting up interviewing procedures, collecting and analyzing data, and making use of the findings within agencies and in the context of broader community planning efforts.

CONA is only one of many assessment models, but it is one that works well and is relatively uncomplicated to implement. The survey instruments and promotional materials found in the appendix can be easily adapted to local conditions. *Sage Guides* are copublished with the Program for Continuing Education in the Human Services of the University of Michigan School of Social Work. Professor Armand Lauffer is series editor.

# INTRODUCTION

The intent of this manual is to provide a practical, usable needs assessment model for community human service agencies. With the exception of an underlying bias toward the consumer-citizen, few conceptual barriers should confront the user. While the model was developed and used within a community mental health context, it is by design practicable for other service settings.

The human service needs assessment model presented here is an outgrowth of over two years of development and revision. It began as a fantasy of a mental health agency's community education committee. It emerged as a coordinated, multiagency research endeavor, initially focusing on a catchment area of well over 200,000 citizens.

The methodology resulted from a cooperative effort between the mental health agency and the research and public service center of a local university. Students participated in the development of the needs assessment as part of this cooperative effort. The purpose of the joint effort was to have undergraduate students, social agency personnel, and university faculty work together in the development and implementation of a human service needs assessment.

The intention of involving students in needs assessment was to assist the local community agency while simultaneously providing the students with a rewarding scholastic experience in an experiential research project. It also made possible a public service to the helping profession in which the students planned to pursue employment. A major portion of the conceptualization, development, and implementation of the Community Oriented Needs Assessment (CONA) Model resulted from the

efforts of junior and senior human services students participating in research courses over a period of eight quarters.
Different students participated each quarter, with one faculty
member consistently responsible.

In the initial planning for the needs assessment, the participants reviewed the literature in the hope of locating an existing
model which could be obtained and replicated with a designated
target population. Most models did not seem to address the
issues of consumerism that were an overriding local concern.
Other models were prohibitively expensive and required en-
gaging private consulting firms. The participants' inability to
locate a financially feasible, acceptable model resulted in staff/
student efforts to generate a methodology to assess human
service needs.

An advisory committee of community social agency represen-
tatives was developed to provide the students with necessary
guidance. Students were asked to address the problem of conducting a needs assessment which would yield usable information. Eleven assessment instruments were generated by the
students. The information used to develop the instruments was
gathered by face-to-face interviews conducted by students with
agency administrators and personnel, boards of directors, and
funding source administrators. The process continued with students initiating a pilot survey to evaluate instruments, sampling
methodology, and interviewing techniques. Revisions of the
model, based on pilot data, resulted in a needs assessment
model which students assisted staff of the mental health center
in implementing. Throughout the needs assessment, students
were intricately involved with agency personnel in making decisions which would ensure the success and effectiveness of the
project. Development and implementation of the model was
accomplished without the benefit of either financial support
from funding sources or designated research personnel. The
staff who developed and implemented the needs assessment
continued to perform services (educational, clinical, administrative) for the agency which employed them.

The financial expenditures were deferred by marketing the needs assessment model and supporting instruments to other mental health agencies. The model has been successfully replicated in disparate catchment areas of a number of mental health clinics.

In the following discussion, the model is presented in a step-by-step fashion to facilitate its use. Each component may be used as stated, or modified to address specific local needs. While some knowledge regarding instrument construction, research design, and statistics is assumed, most human service agencies have this expertise within their staff.

It is our hope that, as in our community, this model will serve as the mechanism for needs assessment, planning, and delivery of more effective human services to the consumer-citizen.

The authors acknowledge those many consumers, potential consumers, and key informants who made the present assessment model a reality. Special recognition is due the undergraduate research students in the Human Services Program at the Delinquency Study and Youth Development Center of Southern Illinois University at Edwardsville, Illinois. During the academic years of 1976 and 1977, these students learned research the exciting way—by doing it. The board of directors and staff of the Mental Health Clinic, Quad City Center, Madison County, Inc., Granite City, Illinois, were concerned and far-sighted enough to recognize the need for assessment data. Without their support, encouragement, and utilization of the data, the process would never have happened. Finally, the authors would like to acknowledge Ms. Susan O'Connor for the skills, expertise, and patience necessary to make a maze of papers into a usable manuscript.

*Chapter 1*

# A HUMAN SERVICES PLANNING MODEL

## GENERAL BACKGROUND

In recent years there has developed an increasing sensitivity to the service needs of the community and a concomitant effort by human service providers to respond more effectively to those needs. One major impetus for this increased sensitivity to community needs has taken the form of federal and state legislation. For example, the passage of Public Law 94-63 in 1975 focused on community mental health centers and the responsibility of those centers to assess and address community needs.[1]

In addition to legislation, community human service agencies have begun to experience the pinch of the impending fiscal crisis in human services. As government funds have diminished, agencies have turned their fiscal attention to potential third party payers such as insurance companies, Medicare, and Medicaid. Increased competition for limited third party funds has coincided with funding source efforts to develop standards for determining which agencies should be eligible to receive third party payment. The apparent intention of this development of standards has been to increase the accountability of agencies providing human services.

One effort to increase accountability of human services to the community has been the process of accreditation. Public

Law 94-63 mandated that the National Institute of Mental Health develop appropriate accreditation standards for mental health agencies. Certain proposed standards seem to be intended to assist human service agencies to meet community needs more effectively.[2] The reality of accreditation, however, is the effect it will have on the survival of community-based human services programs. The key factor is the apparent inevitability that agency accreditation will be directly related to funding, with those agencies which have achieved accreditation being in the best position to receive government and third party funds. The proposal of a national health insurance program is a prime example of one type of third party funding which could be contingent upon accreditation of agencies. In order to survive financially, community agencies must be in a position to qualify for and receive third party and government funds.

The changes necessary for agencies to meet the accreditation standards have also reflected the need for increased community input into service delivery planning and evaluation. As a result of this need for increased community input, there have emerged a number of models for needs assessment.[3]

Early developments in needs assessment seem to have been primarily used to validate, for funding sources, the financial expenditures associated with existing programs and to identify "populations at risk" which should receive allocations for additional programming.[4] Minimal emphasis was placed upon enhancing community participation in planning for service delivery. In most cases, needs assessments were developed to address the pragmatic concerns of accrediting and funding bodies.

In addition to accreditation and funding, the increasing need for a mechanism for community input into human services coincided with an emphasis on consumerism in the marketplace. In the 1960s and 1970s, the visibility of consumer advocates such as Ralph Nader heightened the awareness of individuals as to the impact the consuming public can have on big business. This phenomenon, consumerism, has also begun to invade the human services. Service users and potential users are now, in selected systems, able to shop for services which best suit their needs. An emerging radicalism in the service-consumer population seems to be forcing another look at traditional service delivery mechanisms and programs. One clear result of the consumerism movement has been an overall emphasis on accountability of services and service providers to the public.

The theme which seems to prevail in the discussion of consumerism, accreditation, and funding is an increased responsibility and accountability to the communities which the agency serves. An initial step toward addressing the responsibility and accountability of human services agencies to the community would be the consideration of several conceptual issues. For example: What is the purpose of human services, and what are the goals? How does an agency facilitate and enhance a person's effectiveness in adjusting to a changing self and environment? What kinds of services are really needed? And, indeed, what do we mean by "need" in human services?

When these questions are answered from a global perspective, however, only minimal direction is provided for adapting services to a specific community. It would seem that an agency has a greater likelihood of achieving identified goals by developing a conceptual and operational framework for providing human services based on the perceived goals, needs, and characteristics of the community which the agency serves.

This concern for developing a community-oriented framework for providing human services has escalated the demand for accurate, usable information which reflects the needs and characteristics of a specific population.

The possession of current and reliable information pertaining to human service needs allows for rational decision-making regarding future service needs in a given area. In order to determine priorities of service, it is imperative that agencies and boards of directors possess information from the communities regarding their diffuse and interrelated needs. Data input can provide a basis for program review and revision. The goal of eliminating gaps and redundancies in services can only be approached with reasonably reliable and valid information. It is obvious that without current information about the community, the people within it, and their needs, the effective planning, structuring, and evaluation of programs is more difficult, and the value of programs is clearly reduced.

An effective system of communication between the community and service providers is necessary. Traditionally, service providers have communicated with the consumer by offering programs which reflected staff interest or expertise. The limitations of this approach were obvious, but they were tolerated in view of the fact that no effective method existed for two-way communication between the community and service providers. The present method, the Community Oriented Needs Assessment (CONA) Model, has been developed to enhance two-way communication between the community and service providers.

### THE MODEL

The model is designed to utilize data collected from three sources: demographic/statistical profiles, designated key informants, and individual interviews with randomly selected consumers and potential consumers.

*Demographic statistical profiles.* Information pertaining to human service delivery and areas of public concern can be collected from available public records. Statistical information which can be obtained includes birth rates, death rates, employment data, crime data, mental health center data, data from schools, and so on. Demographic and statistical information is readily available through local and state resources and can be obtained at minimal expense. Demographic and statistical information provides a means for comparison of sample profiles with public record profiles in a given community. In addition, demographic and statistical information provides a basic framework for comparing key informant and consumer perceptions with community reports.

*Key informants.* Key informants are defined as persons having direct contact with individuals experiencing problems in living. Random samples may be drawn from any of a number of relevant informant populations, including bartenders; beauticians; clergy; law enforcement personnel; lawyers; medical doctors; nurses; school administrators; school counselors; school teachers; and social agency personnel. Data collection from key informants can be efficiently accomplished by prepaid mail return of questionnaires circulated by mail, individual contact, and bulk distribution.

Key informants can be asked to provide information on how professionals perceive community problems and need from their vantage point as front-line human service providers. In addition, information can be sought on how referral sources perceive mental health centers.

Data can be gathered, too, regarding ways in which the working relationship between front-line caregivers and mental health service providers could be enhanced.

*Consumer (general public).* Of principal importance in community-oriented needs assessment is consumer data. Consumer data collection can be accomplished by individually interviewing a random sample of the adult population in the geographical area serviced by the agency. To enhance the accuracy of the information collected, the general public should be sampled by a modification of the sampling methodology used by the Survey Research Center at the University of Michigan.[5] This sampling procedure is essentially a stratified, multistage approach which would be expected to result in a relatively low sampling error.

Initially, individual interviewing may be perceived as expensive, time-consuming, and having some degree of risk. Recognizing these limitations, face-to-face interviewing should be used to maximize the expected value of improved community visibility of human service agencies, improved public relations, and of greatest importance, the opportunity to hear from the person whose money supports the services and for whom the services are intended. To assure the quality of face-to-face interviewing, methods should be developed to select and train carefully each interviewer.

The results of individually interviewing a random sample of the general public include data which reflect (1) personal problems and needs; (2) perceived community problems and needs;

(3) the consumer's awareness of available human services and community service providers; and (4) the consumer's attitude toward problems of living and the services designed to assist people in dealing with such problems.

## ADVANTAGES OF THE MODEL

The intended goal of the Community Oriented Needs Assessment Model is to collect data from three discrete and inter-related sources for purposes of comparison and utilization in program planning and evaluation.

One of the greatest advantages of the community-oriented approach is the involvement of consumers in the needs assessment process. A representative sample of the general public is given the opportunity to impact directly on the future service delivery of mental health and other human services in the community. In addition, community volunteers can participate in the interviewing and interviewer training. This experience seems to enhance their knowledge of mental health services and helps them recognize their contribution to the development of the community-based agency.

Community education is a second advantage of the community-oriented model. Information pertaining to the functions and physical plant operations of the community mental health center can be distributed to a wide range of consumers and key informants. The instruments, letters, brochures, and publicity are presented here in a manner which develops an informative, realistic understanding about mental health services. The individual contact with key informants serves as a foundation to improve professional rapport and working relationships.

A third strength of the Community Oriented Needs Assessment Model is that it can be replicated in different geographic locations. Due to extensive model revision and refinement, the efficiency of implementation is quite high. Subsequent replications indicate a continuing downward trend in the amount of time required to apply the model.[6]

The model is designed to be inexpensive and widely applicable. Agency out-of-pocket expenses are generally less than one thousand dollars. Interviewer costs can often be deferred by using as interviewers people who are involved in programs such as the CETA work program. The result is that remaining out-of-pocket expenses include only postal expenditures, printing costs, and the purchase of supplies. The intricacy of the sampling methodology seems to produce a very low error rate, yet the model can be used effectively by nonresearchers, a factor important for most small agencies.

Of the strengths already mentioned, none outweighes the value of the information obtained. Investigators are provided with an extensive data base from which programs can be developed in an effort to meet the needs of specific communities within their service area more effectively. The accuracy of the perceptions of community respondents should be compared with statistical data and key informant perceptions to gain a more definitive understanding of important problems of living in each community. Additionally, a data base is established upon which programs can be planned with longitudinal research, conveniently conducted to evaluate the program effectiveness at meeting the identified community needs.

## APPLICATION OF NEEDS ASSESSMENT DATA

The primary goal of needs assessment is to generate usable information. The primary goal of community-oriented needs assessment is to facilitate community input into human service delivery. The following is an example of how needs assessment information can be incorporated into the service delivery and planning of a mental health agency.

*Defining needed services.* Services have traditionally been developed by an agency staff, perceiving a community need for that service. However, professionals can have a limited perspective regarding the community need, particularly if they do not live in the specific community for which the service is being planned. The information provided by the CONA Model takes much of the guesswork out of community-oriented programming. Statements of actual and perceived community need are available to the program developer, thus enhancing the probability that a given program will address an actual community need.

*Program development.* Having identified a perceived need, the program planner is responsible for establishing a goal for reducing the community need. The next step in the process is to plan the program aimed at accomplishing the identified goal. Community-oriented needs assessment information, which pertains to the community respondents' characteristics and attitudes, can be instrumental in clarifying effective methods for implementing a program in a specific community. For example, needs assessment data on the most effective ways to communicate information to a given population will be essential when efforts are being made to inform the general public about a new program at a minimal expense. Using needs assessment data improves the probability that the program will be successfully implemented in the given community for which it is planned.

*Interagency cooperation.* Agency resources are generally limited, and therefore it is important to choose the most expedient means of meeting a community need.

Community-oriented needs assessment data can be shared with specific human service agencies serving the same geographic area. Community-oriented needs assessment data can be used to identify areas in which cooperative sharing of available services from different agencies can effectively meet a community need, yet avoid the creation of duplicate services. Community-oriented needs assessment data effectively lends itself to the idea of cooperative planning and delivery of human services, a concept too frequently overlooked in the field of human services.

*Funding and accountability.* The CONA Model addresses many of the concerns associated with funding and accountability. First, the data can be used by agency personnel, boards of directors, and funding sources in the analysis of services presently being offered to a community. Second, the data can be used to demonstrate the need and the means for developing specific services in a given catchment area where they may not presently be available. Third, community-oriented needs assessment provides the kinds of information and community involvement required by generally accepted accreditation bodies. Fourth, the assessment can provide a method for accurate program evaluation by reinstituting the survey at a minimal expense after a program has been implemented.

EVALUATION

A methodological system which enables periodic evaluation of the impact of programming on the consumer is a major extension of the CONA Model. Evaluation is less effective if there is no component which provides a way to evaluate future growth. The CONA Model can provide the information needed to assess the effect of what has been implemented, while simultaneously laying the groundwork for future agency growth and development.

SUMMARY

Increased sensitivity and accountability in the arena of human services is mandated by legislation, fiscal constraints, accreditation requirements, and emerging consumerism.

Effective two-way communication between service providers and the community is necessary for sensitivity and accountability. Such communication can occur through the CONA Model.

CONA utilizes data from demographic/statistical profiles, key informants, and consumers or potential consumers.

CONA has the following advantages: It involves consumers; it enhances community education; it is easily transferable; it is relatively inexpensive; and it generates useful data.

Information generated through the CONA Model is useful in defining needed services, in program development, in enhancing interagency cooperation, and in the areas of funding and accountability.

# NOTES

1. See the Community Mental Health Center Amendments, Public Law 94-63, Section 304 (b), Title III, 1975.

2. See the Joint Commission on Accreditation of Hospitals, *Principles for Accreditation of Community Mental Health Service Programs.* Chicago, Illinois, 1975.

3. See Warheit, G. J., Bell, R. A., and Schwab, J. J., *Planning for Change: Needs Assessment Approaches.* University of Florida, Department of Psychiatry, Gainesville, Florida, 1975.

4. See the National Institute of Mental Health, *A Typological Approach To Do Social Area Analysis.* Department of Health, Education and Welfare Publication Number (ADM) 76-262. United States Government Printing Office, Washington, D.C., 1975.

5. A brief description of this methodology may be found in Survey Research Center, Institute for Social Research, *Interviewer's Manual.* University of Michigan Press, Ann Arbor, Michigan, 1976, pp. 35-39.

6. Initial development and application required approximately one and a half years, a second application required approximately six months, and the most recent required approximately two months.

## Chapter 2

## PREASSESSMENT ACTIVITIES

### ORGANIZATION

In order to plan, initiate, and finalize a community-oriented needs assessment, some organizational structure is necessary. Whether it is an existing committee within an agency or, preferably, an interagency consortium, some structure must be identified or developed to assume responsibility for the assessment process. It is desirable to have a consumer, a consumer advocate, or a nonprofessional on this committee. Also, the committee should include some personnel who possess an interest in research methodology. An overriding consideration should be a commitment to more effective consumer-oriented human services.

It is assumed that administration in the agency will be supportive of the assessment process. Given the investment of personnel time and other agency resources needed to conduct a needs assessment, administrative participation is critical. Administrative commitment is also requisite to initiating any program changes dictated by the assessment data.

While an assessment committee and a sympathetic administrator can plan and facilitate the process, the operational responsibility for the research must be delegated to one or two individuals. The designated researchers should be agency staff members and not consultants. The agency workload of the researchers should be reduced or eliminated to allow ample time for this demanding role. The persons selected to be responsible for the research are critical in the eventual success or failure of the project.

## DATA SOURCES

A primary data source in the needs assessment process is public or semipublic records. The demographic and statistical profiles that emerge are invaluable in better understanding the community. The data also provide a framework for comparing information that will be generated from the interviewing and key informant components of the needs assessment.

One approach to needs assessment is based entirely on the use of demographic and similar types of data. *A Typological Approach To Do Social Area Analysis* (NIMH, 1975) is a good reference to review for possible comparative use.[1] Some federal agencies (i.e., Health Service Administration) have used this assessment model and may possibly share data for comparative studies.

An important data source for the assessment researcher is the United States Census.[2] Census documents and reports updating the census tract data are generally available in public libraries. Every local, county, regional, state, and federal agency is required to prepare an annual report that generally contains relevant data for the assessment process. Most of this material is available to the public.

Specific data sources are local and county school districts. Statistics on dropout rates, special education populations, and other relevant variables are available through these units. Local, county, and state law enforcement agencies can provide specific data on number and type of offenses and disposition. The FBI Uniform Crime Reports are another good source of information.[3] The local juvenile court can be an excellent source of data with respect to the juvenile. Most states maintain an office specifically dealing with the aged and the problems of the aged. State departments of mental health, welfare, correction, vocational rehabilitation, health, and so on are excellent data sources to the researcher. Local and regional planning agencies provide unique data with regard to economic issues, land use, mass transportation, economic development, and similar concerns. Most area universities have research data on local concerns generated by faculty researchers.

With a bit of imagination, some manipulation, and very little money (e.g., postage and so on), the needs assessment researcher can develop a superb demographic/statistical profile of the community. In addition to utilizing available data in the needs assessment process, it is important to establish an ongoing mechanism within the agency to obtain and use these data sources. The establishment and monitoring of an agency data bank is well worth the time and effort required.

## ASSESSMENT INSTRUMENTS

General public and key informant instruments must be developed for use in the Community Oriented Needs Assessment Model. The first and primary instrument is an interview schedule developed for face-to-face data gathering from the consumer/general public (see Appendix A, Instrument 1). Additional instruments have to be developed for use with key informants (see Appendix A, Instrument 2). Responses of the key informants and the consumer sample provide the primary data for the needs assessment process.

Sixteen core variables are identified and recommended for inclusion in all instruments. While each instrument can contain items unique to the respondent group, all should contain questions addressing the sixteen core variables. The variables are length of residence in county; race; sex; age; marital status; education; problems in the community; problems in the schools; problems in personal life; the three most serious problems in the community; the best ways to be informed about services; the factors that keep people from seeking help; familiarity with agencies; services that should be expanded; additional services that are needed; proposed new services.

The present instruments and items are designed to be generalizable to other research settings. Further, they are designed to be used with other key informant groups not included in the original research. Items in the instruments can also be modified to address local assessment needs. Prior to initiating item changes, however, the researcher should consult any number of excellent books dealing with this subject.[4]

In analyzing which groups constitute key informants in the community, the needs assessment committee or the researcher may, for example, identify beauticians as a source of data. The changes that are required to modify the key informant instrument are minimal. The core variable items would remain the same, and the word beautician would be substituted for key informant. This type of modification is possible for any key informant group to be surveyed.

Another area of flexibility has to do with the number of key informant groups identified and used in the needs assessment. The key informant groups identified should represent the primary caregivers in the area surveyed. The number of key informant groups selected by the assessment committee or the researcher may vary depending upon local conditions. This change will not significantly affect the overall assessment model.

Some items (questions) in the instruments will require word changes to account for local problems, names, available services, or proposed services. For example, in Item 4 of Instrument 1, General Public, the local county name must be inserted. In Item 21 of the same instrument, other local problems may be substituted for those stated. If the list is changed, the new items should be randomly assigned their order to avoid bias. Item 24 of Instrument 1 should reflect local agency names. Again, random assignment of the names must be done.

Other items that will probably require change are Items 25 and 27 (General Public, Instrument 1). Item 25 seeks to obtain planning input for existing services. The services listed in this item should obviously reflect those available in the agency or agencies conducting the needs assessment. Again, random assignment of choices is necessary. Item 27 relates to proposed services. The time frame ("three years") and the proposed programs are both subject to change to conform with local planning.

Where changes are made in items identified as core variables, the change must be made in all instruments.

## INSTRUMENT FORMAT

While coding and handling of item responses is dealt with in Chapter 4, a brief explanation of the instrument format seems necessary. Instrument 1, General Public needs some explanation. Those parts of the format to be explained are numbered 1 through 8.

&#9312; Interviewer: _____

&#9313; Date of Interview: _____

&#9314; Time of Day: _____

&#9315; Length of Interview (in minutes): _____

&#9316; Sample Area: _____

1. Location of interview?                &#9317; Col. 1: _____

| City | Town | Rural (Be specific) | Township |

2. (If not self-evident, ask:)

   What type of house do you live in?

&#9318; ☐ Single family dwelling *(1)*
   ☐ Duplex *(2)*
   ☐ Apartment *(3)*
   ☐ Mobile Home *(4)*
&#9319; ☐ Other (specify) _____ *(5)*

                                        2: _____

(1) Interviewer: The individual conducting the interview should insert his or her last name or initials in this space. A uniform method should be employed. This information will enable the researcher to check back with the interviewer regarding a questionable response or illegible handwriting, or for field control purposes.

(2) Date of Interview: This information may be helpful when analyzing the data. For example, persons interviewed on the weekend may respond differently than those interviewed during the week. Major local or national events can significantly alter respondent perceptions. Responses prior to and subsequent to such events may be worth noting in the research findings.

(3) Time of Day: The interviewer should indicate morning, afternoon, or evening for the time of day the interview took place. This information will be useful in understanding and interpreting research findings.

(4) Length of Interview: The interviewer should note, with accuracy, the length of each interview in minutes. This is especially important in the initial phases of the interviewing process. It will assist greatly in determining the number of interviewers required and the time frame necessary for completion of this process.

(5) Sample Area: This identifies the specific location where the interview was conducted in terms of "sampling chunks" (see Chapter 4).

(6) Col. 1: This format item relates to keypunching the responses for computer analysis. It refers to the first column in a computer card where the responses will be keypunched.

(7) ☐ Single Family Dwelling *(1)*: The proper box is marked with an "X" indicating the respondent's answer. The number at the end of the respondent's choice is written in that item's column blank. For example, if the respondent selects ☒ Single Family Dwelling *(1)*, the number *(1)* is written in 2: *1*

(8) ☐ Other (specify) _____ *(5)*: This response is for individuals who give answers not accounted for in the space provided.

## PUBLICITY

A major factor in the success or failure of the needs assessment process has to do with publicity. In this context, publicity involves encouraging the public to cooperate in the data collection activities. It also involves ensuring the cooperation of various community agencies.

Presenting information to the public regarding the needs assessment improves respondent cooperation and increases the visibility of the human services agencies involved. Informing the public of the opportunity to impact the human services available in their community serves to broaden public interest in such services.

Identifying the public communication resources is necessary to initiate a public awareness campaign. Popular resources include local and regional newspapers, radio, television, professional newsletters, circulars, and church bulletins. Below is the process for making the public aware of the impending survey research.

*Newspaper.* Local newspapers will generally print public service information without charge. An initial news release should be presented approximately one month prior to beginning the data collection. The initial release should include identification of investigator/agency, statement of purpose, intended procedure, and a means for persons to obtain additional information about the project. (An initial press release example is contained in Appendix B.) Just prior to the start of data collection, a second press release (see Appendix B) should be issued announcing the start of the project. Specifics on purpose, procedure, human rights protection, and public information contacts should be included. A photograph and/or a striking headline improve the chances that the article will be noticed by persons in the community.

*Radio.* Public radio stations are mandated to provide public service announcements without charge. A public service announcement should range between ten and twenty seconds of air time. The accepted method of applying for public service air time is to submit a postcard containing the text of the announcement with a request for date(s) and number of times to be aired. (See Appendix B for an example.) The announcements should reach radio stations two weeks prior to the requested air date(s). A follow-up telephone call to local radio stations will improve the chances of announcements being aired.

An additional means of utilizing radio is to arrange to discuss the project on a radio talk show. Scheduling can generally be arranged by contacting a local radio station and discussing the project with the program director.

*Television.* Television station cooperation can be obtained by means of public service announcements, or by presenting the project as a human interest story on local news telecasts. Television air time is very difficult to obtain, and negotiations should commence four to six weeks in advance of the desired telecast date(s). Contact with stations should be initiated by telephone with the intention of arranging a personal interview. Individual station requirements will dictate how materials should be prepared.

*Key informants.* Information regarding needs assessment surveying is best communicated to human services caregivers by professional bulletins, newsletters, organizational meetings, and pamphlets. Remember that caregivers receive a considerable number of flyers and "junk mail." Keep comments concise in presenting information about the project. Prepare the information in a manner which will catch the glance of someone thumbing through a stack of papers. Having the topic printed in large black letters is one effective means of gaining a key informant's attention.

*Police.* Face-to-face collection of data in a community poses concern for the safety of the respondents and interviewers. Local police departments can assist in reducing risks in face-to-face data collection. Contact established with local police officials prior to starting the project helps local officials understand the purpose and process of the project. To protect effectively those involved in the data gathering process, police departments need to be aware that interviewers will be in their district. Arrangements should be made so potential community respondents can telephone police stations to verify the identity of interviewers. Telephone verification can be accomplished by providing lists of interviewer names to police dispatchers.

Where police are asked to participate as key informants in the survey, the contact with police officials improves questionnaire distribution and response rates.

## ASSURANCE OF HUMAN RIGHTS

Concern for protecting an individual's human rights has become a focal issue for research investigators. Government regulations and legal decisions have encouraged researchers to conduct studies in a manner which in no way inflicts physical or emotional discomfort on participants. Although needs assessment research is generally considered of low risk to participants, maintaining the individual human rights of respondents remains a primary responsibility of the investigator.

*Project review.* The research investigator is urged not to assume that all precautions for the protection of human rights have been achieved by the researcher's methodology. The investigator's best assurance that protection of human rights has been achieved is to have the proposed study reviewed by a committee of qualified peers. An agency or local university may have an approved committee for evaluating such research proposals.

*Informed consent.* One principal means of assuring protection of human rights is to obtain informed consent from the respondents. Informed consent is a written agreement signed by the respondent, expressing willingness to participate. For the purpose of needs assessment research, obtaining informed consent consists of the following:

(1) informing the respondent of his or her right to refuse to answer any question

(2) explaining to the respondent how the information requested will be used

(3) offering to answer any questions the respondent may have concerning the interview

(4) assuring that the respondent's anonymity will be maintained

(5) obtaining the signature of respondent and date of signature on a prepared consent form following completion of the interview

The consent form should be signed at the completion of the interview to ensure that the respondent is aware of what information will be used. (A sample consent form is presented in Appendix C.)

For further information on informed consent, refer to *Department of Health, Education and Welfare Policy on Protection of Human Subjects.* [5]

## SUMMARY

Organization for needs assessment should involve consumer and agency administration involvement.

Sources of existing data, especially in regard to demographics, must be identified.

Instruments to be utilized in collecting data from key informants and consumers must be developed. A core of common variables should be maintained across all instruments. Changes in the sample instruments (see Appendix A) must be made based on local conditions.

The needs assessment effort should be publicized to both consumers and to key informants. Local law enforcement agencies should be made aware of activities.

The assessment procedure must assure the protection of human rights. This can be accomplished through project review and securing informed consent of respondents.

## NOTES

1. See the National Institute of Mental Health, *A Typological Approach To Do Social Area Analysis.* Department of Health, Education and Welfare Publication Number (ADM) 76-262. United States Government Printing Office, Washington, D.C., 1975.

2. See United States Census of Population. United States Government Printing Office, Washington, D.C., 1970.

3. See FBI Uniform Crime Reports, *Crime in the United States, 1975.* Federal Bureau of Investigation, Department of Justice, Washington, D.C., 1976.

4. See Orenstein, A. and Phillips, W.R.F., *Understanding Social Research: An Introduction.* Allyn & Bacon, Boston, Massachusetts, 1978. See also Selltiz, C., Wrightsman, L. S., and Cook, S. W., *Research Methods in Social Relations.* Holt, Rinehart & Winston, New York, 1976.

5. See *Department of Health, Education and Welfare Policy on Protection of Human Subjects.* Department of Health, Education and Welfare, United States Government Printing Office, Washington, D.C., 1971.

*Chapter 3*

## INTERVIEWING PROCEDURES

Information from consumers concerning mental health problems and needs can be gathered through any one of three methods: mailed questionnaires, telephone interviews, or personal interviews. Each of these methods has a number of advantages and disadvantages.[1] For the CONA Model, personal interviews are considered the most useful. This method is preferable, because it permits the collection of complex and extensive responses which cannot be obtained through the other methods. It also avoids the problem of low response rate common to mailed questionnaires and the difficulty of obtaining correct telephone numbers for selected households.

### SELECTION OF INTERVIEWERS

The first step in the interviewer selection process is to make an estimate of the required number of interviews. Information which can be utilized includes the following: (1) actual size of the sample to be interviewed; (2) estimated average time per interview—this should include travel time, time involved in locating the interview site, actual interview time, and time involved in returning to the interview site for those respondents who were not at home the first time; and (3) deadlines for completion of the interviewing process.

For example, let us suppose that 500 interviews are needed and the interviewing must be completed in a month. The average time per interview with the CONA Model is approximately 42 minutes. This includes 30 minutes of actual interviewing time, 5 minutes to locate the specific household to be interviewed, 5 minutes travel time between households, and returning once to one-fifth of the households in order to find someone at home.[2] Based on the figure of 42 minutes per interview, it would require 350 hours to conduct the required number of interviews ($42 \times 500/60 = 350$). Thus more than two (2.2) full-time interviewers working 40 hours a week would be required to complete the interviews in the allotted time ($350/40 \times 4 = 2.19$). In our experience, interviewers are seldom able to work full-time, so this number would have to be adjusted according to the actual time available per interviewer.

Once the approximate number of interviewers required is established, it is necessary to determine the available sources from which the interviewers may be recruited. These sources would include the agency sponsoring the research, public service volunteers, local colleges and universities, community service organizations, and job incentive programs. Based on our experience, it is most productive to seek volunteer interviewers (e.g., an agency administrator requesting volunteers rather than requiring employees to obtain a certain number of interviews).

Determination should be made prior to the recruitment process as to whether volunteers are to be paid. Paying volunteers is highly recommended if financial resources permit. Monetary incentives increase output and commitment of interviewers, as well as providing the investigator with a greater degree of control over interviewer behavior.

The process of selecting specific individuals who will represent the research project as interviewers must be done with considerable care.[3] In a very general sense, both objective and subjective characteristics of potential interviewers should be considered in selection.

Objective characteristics are probably the easiest to assess. Interviewers are likely to find it necessary to work weekends and nights and should be prepared to do so. In most instances, it is necessary for interviewers to have regular access to a car. They should be in good health as interviewing often requires considerable walking, climbing stairs, and so on. They should present a reasonable personal appearance. They should have an adequate command of the English language without extreme regional or ethnic accent. Previous interviewing experience would be helpful. Ideally, the interviewer should be similar to the persons being interviewed in terms of identifiable external characteristics (e.g., race, sex, socioeconomic level, and so on). This helps reduce risks, improves the likelihood of obtaining interviews, and enhances the validity of the data.

Subjective characteristics of the potential interviewer are more difficult to judge, but are probably more important than the objective characteristics. Interviewers must be honest. The investigator is depending on them actually to conduct the interview, ask all questions and accurately record responses. Interviewers must be reliable. They are working, to a large extent, independently and must complete a given task in a limited period of time. Interviewers need to be fairly well-organized and capable of accurately recording a variety of responses. Completed interview schedules must be legible for coding and keypunch purposes. In order to obtain complete interviews, the interviewers must possess a certain degree of "social sense." They must be able to get along with a variety of people who have an even greater variety of ideas, opinions, and beliefs. Finally, interviewers must possess a strong sense of perseverance. Face-to-face interviewing can be a long, discouraging, and often unrewarding process. Interviewers must have enough commitment to and interest in the research to complete a series of interviews despite considerable adversity.

After the selection of the interviewers, it is strongly recommended that the research investigator enter into an agreement (preferably a written agreement) with these individuals. This agreement should clearly delineate the responsibilities of both parties. It should address financial arrangements, training requirements, time and quota commitments, and any inherent legal responsibilities. The agreement will not be legally binding; it will, however, serve to improve commitment and cooperation between investigator and interviewer and lessen the chance for misunderstandings.

## TRAINING OF INTERVIEWERS

Interviewer training can be conducted individually or in groups. Group training is suggested, since less training time is required, and the questions raised in the group session will benefit all in attendance. Training can be completed in one session of approximately three to four hours. Attendance at the entire training session should be mandatory for all interviewers, regardless of previous training or experience.

Prior to or at the beginning of the training session, interviewers should be provided with a packet of information. This packet should contain the following: an agenda for the training session; background information about the research project; tips on interviewing skill development; a copy of the instrument(s); a list of names and telephone numbers of community emergency resources; writing materials; and any other relevant information and materials. Several general areas should be included in the training session itself.[4]

*Background and rationale.* A brief description of the evolution and preparation of the research project will help give interviewers a clearer idea of its nature and importance. The practical usefulness of the information should be stressed. Explaining the project's development is beneficial, because the interviewers will have a better appreciation of why they are being asked to interview. Better understanding will increase their commitment to the project, thus increasing data validity.

*Project goals and objectives.* The trainer should provide clear, specific statements of the purpose of the research and examples of possible outcomes. Information which may cause interviewers to bias the data should be avoided. For example, interviewers should not be told there is an expectation that one racial group will be less willing to participate in the needs assessment than another. This expectation may adversely affect the effort an interviewer expends to get the interview from persons in certain racial groups. Or, in a slightly different example, interviewers should not be told that persons living in one particular area of the city are expected to answer a given question in a certain way. This could affect how the interviewer asks the question and/or records the response when interviewing in the different areas.

The trainer should provide a general explanation of the overall methodology employed in the project. Information on sampling procedures, confidence intervals, data collection, and data analysis will help the interviewers develop a clearer understanding of their role in the research. Developing the feeling that they are a part of a larger effort and understanding the other components of this effort will, again, increase interviewer commitment.

*Administration of the instrument.* An extensive amount of time should be given to going over the questions contained in the instrument with specific instructions on how to administer each particular item and how to record responses to each. Each item should be explained carefully, with some rationale for why the item is included. Emphasis should be placed on ways to avoid bias in an interview.[5] Interviewers should be instructed not to interpret, answer questions, or give examples for respondents since the interviewers' statements may affect how the respondent answers. Interviewers should become quite familiar with the instrument and feel comfortable with its use.

*Interviewing techniques*[6]. The trainer should assume that the interviewers have few skills for interviewing and train accordingly. Four areas of concentration are suggested. First, emphasis should be placed on the importance of physical appearance. Generally, whether or not the interviewer will obtain the interview is determined within the first twenty seconds of contact. Initial impressions, therefore, play a major part in the decision of the respondent. Interviewers should consider how they present themselves in terms of dress, overall appearance, and body language. They should not wear pins, buttons, and so on which identify them with a particular social group or cause. This can distract respondents, lead them to refuse to be interviewed, or cause them to slant their responses a particular way. Interviewing materials should be carried in a folder rather than a briefcase. This reduces the likelihood of the interviewer being perceived as a salesman. The focus should be on becoming aware of how one presents oneself to strangers.

Second, techniques for obtaining the interview should be discussed.[7] This segment should focus on the opening verbal contact between interviewer and respondent. Discussion, role playing, and suggestions for opening statements may be generated. Interviewers should be encouraged to introduce themselves by name. The purpose of the study, the way the respondent was chosen, and the use of the information should be briefly explained. The intent is to build skills which will help both the interviewer and the respondent remain at ease.

Third, communication techniques in interviewing are extremely important. This section of the training is meant to focus on communication skills. Important skills such as proper use of voice, inflection, and responses given in an accepting, affirmative manner will enhance interview contacts. Focus here is on improving interviewers' skills in relating to others through training in specific communication techniques.

Fourth is assertiveness training. An extensive amount has been written on assertiveness training.[8] Time restraints on training prohibit any in depth assertiveness skill development. Some hints, however, on how to be assertive will help the interviewer in face-to-face interview contact. A brief explanation about using positive "I" statements, avoiding questions which can be answered "yes" or "no," and encouraging respondents to consider items fully (particularly open-ended items), generally improves the interviewer's confidence as well as the quality of information obtained. Focus is on helping the interviewer feel a greater sense of potency and competency while interviewing.

*Role playing.* Following the discussion of interviewing techniques, it is beneficial to have interviewers pair off and practice administering the questionnaire to one another. Trainers should make themselves available to answer questions or comment on the techniques of interviewers. The role playing process will serve to familiarize interviewers with the instrument and the process of interviewing. Interviewers should have the opportunity to play the role of both respondent and interviewer. This will give them both perspectives on the various questions and thus provide them with a clearer understanding of what is involved in obtaining responses.

*Additional issues.* Training of interviewers should include an explanation of the importance of the protection of human rights and interviewer safety. The consent form attached to each questionnaire should be explained, with emphasis on its significance. Procedures for obtaining signed consent forms should be provided. Interviewers should be given specific directions for assuring respondents of anonymity in the conflicting context of the signed consent form.

With regard to interviewer safety, the guideline which should be stressed is the interviewer's use of good judgment or "common sense." Interviewers should be instructed to avoid putting themselves at risk under any circumstances. Locations which appear unsavory or dangerous should be avoided and left for the investigator to deal with. The rule of thumb is that no interview is important enough to risk injury to interviewer or respondent. Whenever resources allow, interviewers should be encouraged to work in teams to reduce the risk of personal injury and investigator liability. Interviewers should also be instructed about ways of terminating interviews if the respondent becomes upset or annoyed.

The interviewer should be assured that one of the investigators will always be available upon immediate notice should a problem arise. Interviewers should be provided with a list of telephone numbers for emergency community resources and should be encouraged to use them when appropriate. Time should be allowed for discussion of interviewer concerns about interviewing in the community and the possible difficulties which interviewers may face. The few extra minutes taken during training may help avoid problems later in data collection.

Interviewers should be instructed on how to handle unoccupied residences, those where no one is home, and those where
the resident refuses to be interviewed. If a residence appears to
be unoccupied, the interviewer should confirm this with someone in a position to know (e.g., neighbor, mailman, and so on)
before reporting it as unoccupied. If there is no one home, the
interviewer should be informed whether he is responsible for
returning at a later time or whether he should just report "no
one home." Also, if the interviewer is expected to return, he
should be informed how many times he must do so. Finally, the
interviewer should note any unique identifying characteristics
of the residence if someone else is going to conduct "not at
home" interviews. This will reduce the time required in locating
these residences at a later date.

Interviewers should be cautioned not to insist on an interview
and not to become unpleasant if an individual refuses to give an
interview. Such behavior will generally not lead to an interview,
and if it should, the validity of the resultant data would be
questionable. In addition, it can have a negative effect on public
relations.

The final item of the training agenda is to clarify interviewing
assignments, scheduling, pick-up and return locations, and so
on. These should be made clear to the interviewers. It should be
emphasized that completed interview schedules are to be re-
turned promptly. This reduces the chance of their being lost or
damaged. Also, names will be attached to the completed schedules, and the investigator has an obligation to ensure the
anonymity of respondents.

INTERVIEWER IDENTIFICATION

Before beginning the actual data collection, interviewers
should have complete identification. They should be provided
with identification badges which include a picture. These should
have a signature of authorization from the administrator of the
sponsoring agency. Local police and/or social agencies should be
given a list of interviewer names. Respondents can then be
informed that the identity of an interviewer can be verified

through calling police or designated social agencies. Copies of a letter of introduction (see Appendix D) explaining the purpose of the research and identifying the sponsoring agency should be provided to each of the interviewers. Use of official agency letterhead is suggested. The letter can serve to allay any suspicions a respondent may have; if left with the respondent, it can serve a secondary public relations function by providing members of the community with the agency address and telephone number.

## FIELD CONTROL

In order to ensure integrity in the emerging assessment data, the researcher must plan and operationalize field control mechanisms. There are very specific interviewer-related problems in face-to-face data collection that must be anticipated and addressed. Several references listed at the end of this chapter will serve the researcher well in dealing with field control problems.[9]

It is imperative that the researcher design a method of checking with a percentage of the respondents to determine if they were actually interviewed. While this may imply a questioning of interviewer integrity, it is still necessary in this type of research. One option is a rigorous method of telephoning a predetermined percentage of the sample and asking if they have been interviewed. Individual names will be available from the sample selection source. The need for such field control mechanisms should be explained to the potential interviewers. Generally, this explanation should dissipate most adverse reactions to the process.

Another field control problem is interviewer "burnout." This phenomenon is directly caused by the number of interviews conducted. Burnout occurs with both paid and volunteer interviewers. Essentially, burnout has to do with the boredom, frustration, and tedium resulting from asking the same questions over and over again. Interviewers tend to become abrupt, less personable, and inclined to distort responses. Also, when this phenomenon occurs, transcription of responses becomes shoddy and more difficult to read.

Generally, the researcher can also address this issue during interviewer training. However, support mechanisms, opportunities to restate the importance of the research, and other devices should be planned during data collection.

A final part of field control is the need to have someone available by telephone to respond to needs and problems of the interviewers. It is clearly preferable to have the individual responsible for the overall research project available. If this is not possible, a secretary or volunteer should definitely be available by telephone when interviewers are in the field.

SUMMARY

The use of personal interviews with consumers is recommended.

The number of interviewers necessary to complete the needs assessment in a given period of time must be determined. Interviewers should be selected based on certain criteria, both objective and subjective. A clear work agreement should be reached between the researcher and the selected interviewers.

Interviewer training should include background and rationale for the research, project goals and objectives, instrument administration, techniques of interviewing, and role playing.

Interviewers should be provided with adequate identification before beginning the actual interviewing process.

Adequate field control will ensure data integrity, reduce interviewer burnout, and eliminate many interviewer difficulties.

## NOTES

1. Comparative discussions of mailed questionnaires, telephone interviews, and personal interviews may be found in a number of sources including the following: Black, J. A. and Champion, D. J., *Methods and Issues in Social Research*. John Wiley, New York, 1976, pp. 371-375, 390-391; Hoinville, G., Jowell, R., et al., *Survey Research Practice*. Heinemann, London, 1977, pp. 125-127; Moser, C. A. and Kalton, G., *Survey Methods in Social Investigation*. Basic Books, New York, 1972, pp.

257-262; Nachmias, D. and Nachmias, C., *Research Methods in the Social Sciences.* St. Martin's Press, New York, 1976, pp. 100-109; Orenstein, A. and Phillips, W.R.F., *Understanding Social Research: An Introduction.* Allyn & Bacon, Boston, Massachusetts, 1978, pp. 227-230; Selltiz, C., Wrightsman, L. S., and Cook, S. W., *Research Methods in Social Relations.* Holt, Rinehart & Winston, New York, 1976, pp. 294-299; and Tuch Farber, A. J. and Klecka, W. R., *Random Digit Dialing.* Police Foundation, Cincinnati, Ohio, 1976, pp. 13-17.

2. Specific computation are as follows:

Actual interviewing time $500 \times 30 = 15000$ minutes
Location time $\quad\quad\quad\quad 500 \times 5 \;=\; 2500$ minutes
Initial travel time $\quad\quad\; 500 \times 5 \;=\; 2500$ minutes
Return travel time $\quad\; 100 \times 10 =\; 1000$ minutes

$\Sigma$ time $= 21000$ minutes

Mean $\times$ time/interview $= 21000/500 = 42$ minutes

3. Detailed discussion of interviewer selection may be found in the following: Black and Champion, *op. cit.,* pp. 360-361; Hoinville and Jowell, *op. cit.,* pp. 106-110; Moser and Kalton, *op. cit.,* pp. 282-287; and Warwick, D. P. and Lininger, C. A., *The Sample Survey: Theory and Practice.* McGraw-Hill, New York, 1975, pp. 222-224.

4. A general discussion of interviewer training may be found in Moser and Kalton, *op. cit.,* pp. 287-291. Warwick and Lininger, *op. cit.,* pp. 224-229, provide a detailed outline of a quite thorough interviewer training program.

5. An extensive discussion of sources of bias in interviewing may be found in Hyman, H. H., *Interviewing in Social Research.* Chicago, Illinois, University of Chicago Press, 1954. Orenstein and Phillips, *op. cit.,* pp. 230-245, and Warwick and Lininger, *op. cit.,* pp. 199-202, provide much briefer discussions of this topic.

6. Selltiz, Wrightsman, and Cook, *op. cit.,* pp. 563-573, provide a very good discussion of the role of the interviewer in terms of what he must accomplish. The interviewer must have at his disposal techniques adequate for the demands of his role.

7. Warwick and Lininger, *op. cit.,* pp. 208-209, provide a useful discussion of how to deal with commonly encountered resistance to being interviewed.

8. Following is a brief list of assertiveness training books. It is by no means exhaustive of the good assertiveness training books available. Alberti, R. and Emmons, M., *Stand Up, Speak Out, Talk Back!* Pocket Books, New York, 1975; Alberti, R. and Emmons, M., *Your Perfect Right.* Impact, Fredericksberg, Virginia, 1974; Bloom, L., Coburn, K., and Pearlman, J. *The New Assertive Woman.* Dell Publishers, New York, 1975; Lange, A. J. and Jakubowski, P., *Responsible Assertive Behavior: Cognitive/Behavioral Procedures for Trainers.* Research Press, Champaign, Illinois, 1976; Smith, M. J. *When I Say No, I Feel Guilty.* Dial Press, New York, 1975.

9. Discussions concerning field control problems may be found in a number of sources including the following: Hoinville, G. and Jowell, R., *op. cit.,* pp. 115-123; Cannell, G. F., Lawson, S., and Hauser, D., *A Technique for Evaluating Interviewers Performance.* Survey Research Center, University of Michigan, Ann Arbor, Michigan, 1975, pp. 31-42; Survey Research Center, Institute for Social Research, *Interviewer's Manual.* University of Michigan Press, Ann Arbor, Michigan, 1976, pp. 114-115, 120.

*Chapter 4*

## DATA COLLECTION AND ANALYSIS

As discussed in Chapters 1 and 2, three types of data relevant to the purposes of needs assessment should be collected. Demographic information pertinent to the geographical area of interest is necessary to provide baseline data regarding population characteristics and general community problems. Such data can also be useful in developing social and physical profiles of the area.

Information from key informants enables consideration of the opinions of front-line human service providers. This type of data provides important information concerning agency caregivers' opinions and beliefs about needed human services.

The final type of data is gathered in face-to-face interviews with residents of the area of interest. This data comprises the heart of the consumer-oriented needs assessment process. Such information is vital in specifying any number of concerns and issues, including awareness of existing services, perceptions of existing services, and perceived needs and problems.

These three types of data each provide useful information by themselves and can be considered independently. In addition, various combinations of the three types can be invaluable when studying certain issues and concerns.

## DEMOGRAPHIC INFORMATION

Information pertaining to delivery of human services and to areas of public concern is readily available through a number of public sources. Information on rates of birth, death, marriage, and divorce is available through local government agencies and from census data. Information concerning crime and related issues is available through law enforcement agencies. In order to avoid being overwhelmed by the amount of information available, the investigator should have a clear idea of the data required. It is also imperative to formulate the research question carefully if demographic data is to be employed in developing an answer. The question should be framed so that available statistical records can provide an answer. Unlike most research methods, in which the data are collected for the specific purpose of providing an answer, the data here exist before the questions.[1] A listing of types and sources of demographic data is found in Appendix E.

## KEY INFORMANT DATA COLLECTION

The initial task in key informant data collection is the selection of the key informant populations to be surveyed. Key informants for human services needs assessment can be defined as persons having direct contact with individuals experiencing "problems of living." The following are persons in professions which meet the key informant selection criteria: clergy, community officials, law enforcement officials, law enforcement personnel, lawyers, medical doctors, nurses, school administrators, school counselors, school teachers, social agency personnel, and so on.

The second step is to develop listings of names and addresses of the population in each key informant category. At this point, the investigator will need to determine what portion of each key informant population will comprise the research sample. The determination of sample size is dependent upon available physical and monetary resources. Whenever feasible, it is suggested that as large a proportion (if not all) of the population be sampled as possible. When sample size does not equal population size, the samples should be selected from the population by an accepted random selection process.

In most instances, listings of each key informant population are available from various sources (e.g., lawyers from the local bar association, school personnel from the local school district directory, and so forth). These lists can then provide a basis for sampling. Assuming the names on a list are not arranged in an order which has bearing on the content of the responses which are given, a systematic sample is probably the most efficient sampling procedure. This is easier and more convenient than a simple random sample, while providing comparable accuracy. In a systematic sample, every Kth name from the list is selected where K is equal to the population size divided by the desired sample size. The first name is chosen by randomly selecting a number between 1 and K.[2]

After the sample is selected, the next step is the actual data collection. This may be done through face-to-face interviews or through the distribution of questionnaires to the individuals selected in the sample. Based on experience with the CONA Model, the distribution of questionnaires appears to be an adequate mode of data collection for most populations of key informants, in terms of response rates and completeness of responses. Possible exceptions to the rule are lawyers and law enforcement personnel.[3] For these groups, personal interviews may be required.

Assuming questionnaires are to be used, questionnaire packets must be prepared. These should include a copy of the appropriate questionnaire, a letter explaining project intentions and what is expected of the respondent (see Appendix D), and a self-addressed prepaid return envelope.

Three methods for distributing questionnaire packets are suggested: mail distribution, individual distribution, and bulk distribution.

*Mail distribution.* Questionnaire packets can be mailed directly to key informants. First-class postage is recommended to ensure that the envelope is not put aside as "junk mail." Mail distribution is convenient, but generally expensive.[4]

*Individual distribution.* Where inexpensive manpower is available (students, volunteers) questionnaires can be delivered directly to the offices of key informants. Three advantages are gained from individual distribution. First, postage expenditures are reduced. Second, public relations and professional rapport are improved. Third, the likelihood of return is improved when the personal contact is extended.

*Bulk distribution.* The needs assessment research conducted by the authors indicates that return rate is not adversely affected by bulk distribution of questionnaire packets. Large quantities of questionnaire packets can be distributed through organizational administrators to nurses, social agency personnel, law enforcement personnel, and school personnel. By obtaining the cooperation of administrators, questionnaires can be distributed to identified groups or specific individuals without postal expenditure.

PERSONAL INTERVIEWS

Personal interviews involve collecting data from a random sample of consumers or potential consumers of human services. Face-to-face interviewing is time-consuming and carries some degree of risk. These limitations, however, do not outweigh the value of the information collected.

Some advantages of face-to-face interviewing include improved community visibility of human services agencies, improved public relations, and most important, the opportunity to hear directly from the people whose money supports the services and who needs the services are intended to serve. Consumer input into human service planning is the "payoff" of face-to-face data collection.

Several sampling methodologies have been developed for needs assessment research.[5] The ultimate purpose of the sampling is to obtain a representative sample of a population. The selection of a probability sample enables the specification of the degree of error involved in generalizing from sample data to population parameters. The probability of a given degree of error can be identified *only* if the sample is a probability sample. A probability sample is one in which each element or member of the population has some specifiable, greater-than-zero chance of being included in the sample. Thus, efforts should be directed toward obtaining a probability sample of residents in the area of interest.

The suggested sampling procedure is a modification of the model used by the Survey Research Center of the University of Michigan in its national surveys.[6] This model is basically a stratified, multistage procedure.

The first step is to estimate the total population age 18 and over in the geographic area of interest.[7] This can be done from the most currently available census data. The population figures must then be increased by a given amount to account for growth (or decreased to account for decline) since the time the census data was collected. Estimates of the appropriate increase or decrease may be obtained from various local planning agencies. This figure then becomes the population size (N).

From a strictly sampling point of view, the size of the sample is determined by the variability of characteristics of interest in the population. A definite sample size can be decided upon only if the desired probable accuracy of the results and the proportion or variance for responses to given items by the population is known.[8] In actual practice, the proportion or variance in the population is not normally known. Thus, under normal circumstances, the size of the sample to be interviewed is based on a number of considerations: specifically, the degree of error, the cost, and the amount of time involved. Based on these factors, the final sample size (n) can be set. This figure should permit a reasonably small degree of error and yet not involve excessive cost or time.[9]

The next step involves the computation of the "sampling fraction." The sampling fraction, then, will be used to specify certain areas to be included in the sample. In its most basic form, the sampling fraction (f) is equal to the sample size (n) divided by the population sice (N). This basic form, however, must be adjusted by the coverage rate (CR) or the number of households the interviewer can locate, the occupancy rate (OR) or the number of occupied housing units, and the response rate (RR) or the number of persons willing to respond. Based on numerous previous surveys, realistic rates for these factors are CR = .95, OR = .98, and RR = .75. Computation of the adjusted sampling fraction permits specification of the number of interviews which must be attempted in order to obtain the desired sample size. The formula for the adjusted sampling fraction is as follows:

$$f = \frac{n}{(N) \ (CR) \ (OR) \ (RR)}$$

where:   n = sample size
         N = population size
        CR = coverage rate
        OR = occupancy rate
        RR = response rate

After this is computed, it can then be divided into N in order to obtain the number of interviews which must be attempted in order to attain n. This adjusted number of interviews is N'.

The next step in the procedure involves stratification of the area of interest. Stratification should be based on variables which are relevant to the purpose of the survey. If this is done, error will be reduced. Possible variables include race, economic factors, and a rural-urban dimension. It is generally most desirable to define the strata geographically by clearly identifiable boundaries, such as city limits. Often there are subdivisions, groups of houses, or even individual homes near or immediately adjacent to a given city but outside city limits. When these are clearly of a nonrural nature, they can be included in the stratum represented by the city. Clearly rural areas can be combined into a rural stratum even though such areas are separated geographically.

After stratification, it is necessary to develop a sample frame, or a listing of all housing units in each of the strata. Housing units are more convenient to use as the basic sampling elements than individuals. Sample frames can be developed through the use of current city directories, county highway maps (which show the location of dwellings), mapping by the investigators, and any other available sources.

Once a suitable sample frame is developed for each of the strata, a "chunking" procedure can be performed. This involves breaking each stratum down into smaller sections or "chunks" consisting of a number of housing units located in close proximity to each other. The number of housing units placed in a "chunk" depends largely on the housing density (the greater the density, the larger the "chunks" are in terms of number of housing units). Normally a range of twelve to twenty housing units per "chunk" is adequate for all but the most or least densely populated areas. The same range of number of housing units per "chunk" should be used for all strata. A list of "chunks" and the number of housing units in each should be developed for each of the strata.

The previously computed sampling fraction can then be applied to the list of "chunks" within strata in order to select specific "chunks" from which housing units will be selected for interviewing. This involves selecting every "chunk" which has a K$th$ element in it, where K equals the sampling fraction. The procedure is to select randomly a number between 1 and K, and then to count the housing units in the list of "chunks" for a given stratum until this K$th$ housing unit is reached. The "chunk" containing this housing unit is then the first "chunk" selected. Starting with the next "chunk" and counting until K is reached yields the second "chunk" and so on, until the stratum is exhausted. This is done for each stratum. The end result is a relatively small number of selected "chunks" for each stratum.

The next step is to check the selected "chunks."[10] This involves actually going to each of the selected "chunks" and making certain they contain the housing units they are thought to contain. New Housing units should be added, and no longer existing ones should be removed.

After the "chunks" have been checked and brought up to date, the final selection of housing units can be performed. The first step is to determine how many housing units should be chosen from each of the selected "chunks." This is given by dividing the number of selected "chunks" into the previously computed adjusted sample size or n. If this is not a whole number, it is better to round up unless it exceeds a whole number by a very insignificant amount. Rounding up helps to ensure that sufficient interview locations are approached in order to attain the desired number of interviews. The second step is to select (using random number tables) the required number of housing units from each of the selected "chunks." This involves numbering the housing units within "chunks," reading down the column of random numbers, and selecting the required number of housing units based on the random numbers which are less than or equal to the total number of housing units in a given "chunk."

This entire sampling procedure results in a probability sample of a given area. It also permits identification of specific housing units for interviewing. Interviewers know exactly which housing units to contact and do not make arbitrary choices of their own. (A detailed example of this sampling procedure is contained in Appendix F.)

DATA ANALYSIS

Data may be compiled manually or through computer processing. In the interest of efficiency, computer processing is strongly recommended. The bulk of the data collected from key informants and through personal interviews may be directly transcribed for keypunching and later computer processing. Responses to open-ended items must be categorized through contact-analysis before they can be processed by computer.[11]

After all the data has been punched, a wide variety of analysis may be conducted. Frequency counts of responses, either for all respondents or for specific subgroups (e.g., strata, a given group of key informants, and so on) can be made. Various comparisons on the core variables discussed in Chapter 2 may be made between the different subgroups or combinations of subgroups. Comparison of responses to sets of items can be made within a given group of respondents. There are a variety of existing computer packages which are more than adequate to do these types of analyses with the kind of data generated by the present procedures.[12] (A detailed example of the actual use of the data is contained in Appendix G.)

## SUMMARY

Demographic data should be carefully delimited, and the question being asked should be posed in such manner as permits it to be answered by such data.

Relevant key informant groups must be identified, and listings of membership developed to serve as the basis for sampling. After the key informant sample is selected, data must be collected, preferably through the use of questionnaires.

A probability sample of the consumer population must be obtained. This involves deciding on a sample size, computing the "sampling fraction," stratifying, developing a sample frame, "chunking," selecting and checking the "chunks," and selecting housing units.

Computer processing can greatly facilitate the compilation and analysis of data, and it is strongly recommended.

## NOTES

1. Discussion of the use of secondary data sources may be found in Black, J. A. and Champion, D. J., *Methods and Issues in Social Research*. John Wiley, New York, 1976, pp. 418-421; Selltiz, D., Wrightsman, L. S., and Cook, S. W., *Research Methods in Social Relations*. Holt, Rinehart & Winston, New York, 1976, pp. 372-381.

2. For example, a hypothetical population includes 500 lawyers in a given area, and it is determined that 50 of these will be included in the sample.

$$K = N/n$$

$$K = 500/50$$

$$K = 10$$

A random number between 1 and 10 is thus selected, e.g., 7. The 7th name on the list is then included in the sample, as is the 17th, the 27th, and so forth to number 497.

3. Response rates for key informant populations based on questionnaire distribution were as follows:

| Key Informant Group | Range of Response Rates | Mean X Response Rate |
|---|---|---|
| School Administrators | 50-77% | 60% |
| School Counselors | 25-58% | 42% |
| Medical Doctors | 18-50% | 37% |
| School Teachers' | 27-46% | 34% |
| Clergy | 24-49% | 33% |
| Nurses | 22-41% | 32% |
| Social Agency Personnel | 19-51% | 32% |
| Lawyers | 15-40% | 31% |
| Law Enforcement | 15-48% | 27% |

4. When the expected number of responses is high (500 +), it is economically advantageous to negotiate a first-class business reply permit with local post office officials. For example, if questionnaire packets are to be sent to 2000 respondents, it would cost approximately $300 in postage to put a first-class stamp on each return mail envelope. With an estimated 25% return, the researcher would expect to receive 500 questionnaires back from respondents. At current postal rates, a business reply permit would cost $30 for the permit, $75 for an accounting fee, and approximately 16.5¢ for each questionnaire returned. Assuming 500 returns out of 2000 respondents, the total fee using the business reply stamp would be $187.50. Therefore, the approximate savings from using the business reply stamp is $112.50.

5. See Warheit, G. J., Bell, R. A., and Schwab, J. J., *Planning for Change: Needs Assessment Approaches.* University of Florida, Department of Psychiatry, Gainesville, Florida, 1975.

6. This model is described in the Survey Research Center, Institute for Social Research, *Interviewer's Manual.* University of Michigan Press, Ann Arbor, Michigan, 1976, pp. 35-39. A detailed description of sampling theory and procedures can be found in Kish, L., *Survey Sampling.* John Wiley, New York, 1965.

7. Age 18 is used as a minimum, because it is felt that persons below this age would have neither interest nor information relevant to the needs assessment.

8. Appropriate formulae are:

For a proportion     $n = \dfrac{p\,(1-p)}{SE^2}$

where                    n = sample size
                             p = proportion
                             SE = standard error or accuracy

For a mean $\qquad n = \dfrac{\sigma^2}{SE^2}$

where $\qquad$ n = sample size
$\qquad\qquad \sigma^2$ = variance
$\qquad\qquad$ SE = standard error or accuracy

9. Additional discussion of sample size may be found in Moser, C. A. and Kalton, G., *Survey Methods in Social Investigation.* Basic Books, New York, 1972, pp. 146-152; and Warwick, D. P. and Lininger, C. A., *The Sample Survey: Theory and Practice.* McGraw-Hill, New York, 1975, pp. 92-94.

10. "Chunks" in areas likely to be undergoing rapid change (e.g., building, urban renewal, and so on) should be checked before the final selection of "chunks" is made.

11. A good discussion of content analysis, including an interjudge reliability coefficient for nominal data may be found in Scott, W. A. and Wertheimer, M., *Introduction to Psychological Research.* John Wiley, New York, 1962, pp. 183-196.

12. OSIRIS, developed by the Institute for Social Research, University of Michigan and the Inter-University Consortium for Political Research, is one example. SPSS (Statistical Package for the Social Sciences) is another. See Nie, N. H. et al., *SPSS.* McGraw-Hill, New York, 1975.

*Chapter 5*

## INTRA-AGENCY UTILIZATION OF
## NEEDS ASSESSMENT DATA

The general purpose in conducting needs assessment is to enhance a particular human service delivery system. Collection and analysis of accurate data is only the initial phase in completing a comprehensive needs assessment. The factor which determines the usefulness of needs assessment methodology is *how* the raw data is used to impact on the human service delivery system.

The community-oriented needs assessment methodology identifies the consumer as the focal point for determining what type of information is wanted and how the information is to be collected. To maintain a focus on the consumer, the following planning model has been developed for internal agency use of needs assessment data.

The Consumer/Provider Communication (CPC) Model is based on the premise that human services are developed for, supported by, and provided to the general public. Therefore, the general public should have direct input in the planning of human services. The CPC Model is designed to use needs assessment as a communication medium between consumers and service providers.

Needs assessment technology provides a viable means for consumers' concerns and needs to be transmitted to service providers. With the CPC Model, the responses given by consumers and key informants to needs assessment questions can directly impact on planning and evaluating of the service delivery process. The service delivery process can be conceptualized as cyclical, beginning with the identification of a need and continuing through the evaluation of a program designed to meet that need. The process of service delivery is illustrated in Figure 1.

In the CPC Model, consumers are considered the focal point in the service delivery process. Needs assessment functions as an informational link between consumers and the service providers

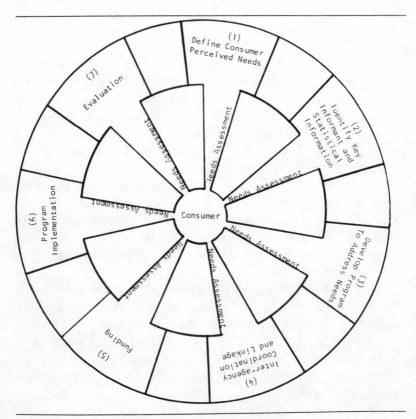

FIGURE 1   Consumer/Provider Communication Wheel

## CYCLE OF SERVICE DELIVERY

*Defining perceived consumer problems (needs).* The initial phase in the service delivery process is defining the specific problem (need) areas perceived by consumers. Accurate consumer needs assessment data provides a framework for clarifying perceived needs specific to a designated population. The service provider can identify a specific area of concern from which to begin program development. Each needs assessment survey question provides information about respondent concerns. A brief scan of the summarized data results in the identification of several themes or issues of concern to consumers. For example, if a large percentage of respondents from a particular stratum chose "problems raising children" in response to the question concerning the most serious problems in their community, and they also indicated "help with raising children" as a popular choice for suggested expansion of services, the investigator could identify childrearing as an issue of concern. Further, support for identifying a particular issue of concern could be obtained by exploring consumer responses to other needs assessment items such as the open-ended questions on neighborhood, community, school, and personal problems. The expected result of needs assessment data analysis would be a prioritized list of identified issues concerning the general public. These ranked issues provide the initial framework to begin planning services for that geographic area.

*Key informant and statistical profile comparisons.* The perceptions of the general public can potentially be influenced by sensation-seeking media, rumor, and incomplete information. To reduce the effect of biased perceptions on service delivery planning, the CPC Model recommends extraction of data from statistical records and key informants to verify perceived general public needs. Demographic profiles offer a statistical reflection of community problems. Key informant needs assessment information provides indicators of consumer needs from the perspective of front-line caregivers. Utilizing key informant and demographic information to validate perceived consumer needs increases the probability that a proposed program will address issues of highest priority. For example, if childrearing is identified as the highest priority consumer issue of concern, the investigator/planner can verify this concern by reviewing key informant needs assessment responses. This will allow him to determine the degree of concern placed on childrearing by different front-line service providers. In addition, statistical records of child-related problems in the community could also assist planners in substantiating general public perceptions and identifying factors relating to the severity of any particular childrearing problems.

The prioritized concerns obtained from key informant needs assessment data and statistical profiles, when combined with general public perceptions, can provide the target issue for developing programs with the greatest likelihood of reducing consumer needs.

*Program developments.* Once a consumer need has been clearly established, the provider is responsible for developing a program to reduce the identified need. Needs assessment data can be valuable in the selection of program design. The responses to needs assessment items represent community attitudes and values. Designing a program consistent with these community values can increase the chances that the program will be accepted by the community. For example, a community which responds favorably to self-help group alternatives and negatively to counseling alternatives would be more likely to accept and use family life education classes than a new family counseling center.

*Interagency coordination and linkage.* In any geographic area, there are a variety of agencies responsible for providing a range of human services. As a program is developed to address a consumer need, efforts should be made to avoid duplicating services already available. Coordinating and linking relevant service providers to meet an identified consumer need is generally economically advantageous. Planners occasionally make the unfortunate error of assuming that a program can only be effective if one agency is involved. Unfortunately, due to competition for funds, territorial disputes, personality conflicts, and other factors, some cooperative efforts do fail.

Needs assessment data is a tool which can be used to bridge some gaps between providers. If the needs assessment survey has been a multiagency endeavor, the framework then exists for cooperative use of the data to address consumer needs. Where the needs assessment has been a single agency production, that data statistically reflects the attitudes of consumers, not the whims of a particular agency staff or administration. When efficient service delivery is the issue rather than territoriality or agency notoriety, efficient cooperative planning allows agencies partially to circumvent the problem of diminishing financial resources.

*Funding.* As a coordinated program plan emerges to address a specific need, the provider confronts the fiscal realities of implementing the program. Funds are consumer funds, allocated frugally through a politically sensitive bureaucracy. Politicians are motivated by the voice of voters and react to proposals which represent the opinions of their constituents. Program planning, based on accurate needs assessment data and statistically supported by that data, is difficult to overlook. Data is available to demonstrate the need and to support the suggested programming strategy for reducing that need.

In certain instances, the available funds for programming may be fixed. The priorities of consumers can provide direction for financial decision-making, reallocating funds to more serve consumers more effectively.

*Program implementation.* The effectiveness of new programming is largely influenced by the effectiveness of the system used to inform the general public of that program's existence. A framework for developing a successful community education/public relations campaign can be obtained by finding out what means of public communication citizens most often use. Gathering such information is one way in which needs assessment can be utilized to implement a program. For example, needs assessment questions on how respondents use media and what media they use most often could suggest the means to inform the public of a new program.

A second way of using needs assessment for program implementation is to illustrate openly to the general public through newspaper articles and public forums how their responses to survey items were used—specifically, how their responses were used to develop the program according to the CPC Model. The provider can seize the opportunity to demonstrate the agency's accountability and responsiveness to consumers.

*Evaluation.* Obtaining information which evaluates how effectively programming has reduced the identified need is the final stage in the service delivery process. Consumer-oriented service planning is most effectively evaluated by consumers. Periodically reassessing the general public with statistically reliable questions enables the planner and provider to determine the impact programming has had on reducing the identified need.

In addition, using needs assessment to evaluate a program creates an opportunity for consumers to establish new needs priorities and perpetuate the service delivery planning process.

CONCLUSION

In the human service provider's efforts to be more accountable to the general public, which both utilizes and funds the services, it is imperative that a system be devised to ensure direct consumer input in the planning and delivery of human services. The Consumer/Provider Communication Model offers a practical informational exchange system between consumers and providers, utilizing needs assessment technology. Systematic program planning and evaluation, based on identified consumer needs, has the greatest potential for efficiently and effectively utilizing limited resources to reduce human needs.

SUMMARY

The Consumer/Provider Communication Model uses needs assessment as a communication medium between consumers and service providers. Needs assessment information can then directly impact on planning and evaluation of the various services to be delivered to the community and consumers.

The service delivery cycle includes a number of phases: The definition of perceived consumer problems; key informant and statistical profile comparison; program development; interagency coordination and linkage; funding; program implementation; and evaluation. Needs assessment data contributes to each of these phases.

*Chapter 6*

# SYSTEMS PLANNING AND NEEDS ASSESSMENT

Previous chapters have offered a method for obtaining needs assessment data and an interagency model for using the information for service delivery planning. The needs assessment process and data obtained are also useful on a broader scale. Human service planning and evaluation goes beyond the scope of an agency's internal structure. Each agency functions as one unit in a complex human service delivery network, which includes other social service agencies, planners, funding bodies, front-line caregivers, and consumers.

Federal regulations for the Comprehensive Community Mental Health Centers Act (1975) and Title XX of the Social Security Act (1974, 1976) mandated state and local planning for mental health and social services. In addition, these regulations introduced the necessity of service evaluation as an integral part of the administration of mental health and social service organizations.[1]

Planning and evaluation are conceptually related processes in the management of complex organizations. Planning involves the rational analysis of information with a focus on (1) setting goals and priorities, and (2) directing decision-making which pertains to the delivery of services. Evaluation involves measuring the degree to which the operationalized definitions of the organization goals are met.

A major tenet of the community mental health movement is that the allocation of services be based on the needs of the community. Therefore, objective information about the community being served is a necessity. In an age of limited resources, community mental health programs must be able to substantiate need and assure the community that they are utilizing the available resources in the most effective and efficient manner. Increased burden is placed on boards of directors and administrators to distribute resources effectively while holding costs down. Additional funding can be contingent upon the administration's ability to offer cost-efficient services.

Information obtained through the CONA Model can be used to educate legislators, human service organizations, board members, and agency staffs about the needs, problems, and concerns of consumers. Sensitizing these groups to expressed needs facilitates awareness of target issues and assists in the development of new approaches for coordinating services and developing programs to meet the identified needs.

PLANNING

Conceptually, the community mental health center embodies community control of local programming and service delivery. This control, in many centers, is exercised through the designation of a board of directors or trustees, which is held accountable to the community and its funding sources for program performance.

Important and difficult board responsibilities include service delivery planning, developing program policy, and allocating resources. Experience indicates that these areas of responsibility are not well-defined; in practice, few boards actually develop policy in a formal, explicit manner.

The CONA Model relates to several areas of the board's responsibilities regarding planning, policy development, community control, and accountability. First, the CONA Model brings to the board "objective" citizen perception of needed available services. With this input, the board's ability to respond to the community is extensively expanded. The board can begin to plan mental health services based on the needs and wants of the consumer-citizen. Second, the board has available the mechanism for (1) reporting to the community, in a comprehensible manner, the services which are currently available; and (2) planning in a rational, objective, and systematic manner for those services which are not. The model which follows has been developed to address the issue of community-based service delivery planning.

COMMUNITY IMPACT PLANNING MODEL

This model for planning with needs assessment information provides examples of how the data can be analyzed and processed for planning. The Community Impact Planning (CIP) Model describes the flow of planning input and responsibility which begins at the consumer level, continues through single and multiple agency levels, and ultimately reaches regional and state planning bodies (see Figure 2). The model provides for consumer and key informant participation and places the planning and evaluating activities at the grass-roots level. Consultation and expertise from management and line staff facilitate the efforts generated by the community.

*Community advisory committees.* The members of community advisory committees represent the community in which they live and/or work. They are responsible for monitoring and evaluating local service interventions, and the reassessment of community need on an ongoing basis. The advisory committees provide an opportunity for consumer participation in local programming and are accountable to the community as well as the agency planning committee and board of directors.

When appointed by the board of directors, the community advisory committee can further legitimize the agency's local program. The membership of the community advisory committee is an important factor; it should consist of key informants from the community, local agency staff, board members, and

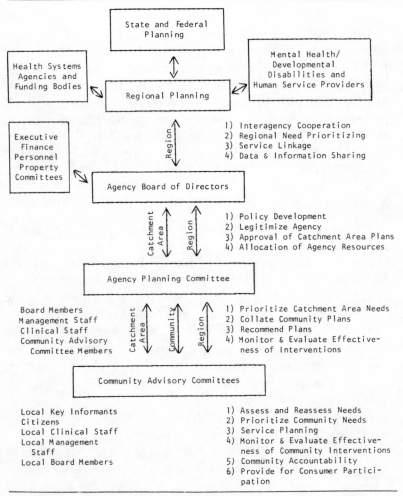

FIGURE 2   Community Impact Planning Model

consumers or potential consumers of the local services. This membership encourages broad representation, continuity of planning, and integration of service delivery.

*Board of directors.* The board of directors is responsible for reviewing and approving the catchment area plans recommended by the agency planning committee, developing related policies, and allocating the necessary resources to ensure the planned interventions. In addition, the board may participate in cooperative regional planning and information sharing to enhance the development of services most efficiently operated on a regional level.

*Regional planning.* Interagency planning, a long-standing problem among the human services, is becoming a major issue as resources become limited and accrediting bodies set standards. The board of directors, through its administrator, must begin to share the information it has about community needs in an effort to enhance funding, link services, and maximize utilization of available resources. Service agency cooperation done locally, as well as regionally, maximizes already existing resources and reduces the gaps in service which affect consumers. The inclusion of major funding sources and governmental planning bodies enhances the likelihood of accomplishing the goal of efficient, effective service delivery planning.

Communities in need of services provided elsewhere can make these needs known and facilitate the development of services in their areas. Staff sharing of specific skills between agencies will enhance the services of agencies to their target populations at a cost lower than full-time staff in some cases.

The sharing of agency skills through interagency staff development and in-service activities can also enhance staff skill levels, broadening the base of services through the local and regional areas. Through sharing data, staff skills, facilities, and services, agencies can delivery a higher quality of service to a broader group of clients, reducing service gaps with linkage agreements and referral procedures.

Funding sources require proof of need, and legislators are beginning to wonder if the enormous expenditure of tax money is having any impact. Data from the CONA Model and plans developed by the community advisory committees will provide needs data and grass-roots support for funding requests. The compilation of supportive information gathered from citizens provides agencies with the ability to demonstrate the need for programming to conservative funding sources. In addition, the mechanisms for evaluation can be used to substantiate the effectiveness of services in support of new funding and refunding of planned services.

## EVALUATION

Once plans have been approved and resources allocated by the board of directors, the mechanisms are in place to evaluate the effectiveness of the planning and service delivery efforts. Through evaluation, the board and administration can gain information about the appropriateness of plans and the need to reallocate resources and replan interventions.

Evaluation examines the services currently delivered, using the information about the community needs and the agency's objectives. The needs assessment process can be used to establish a baseline of community needs. After the interventions have been carried out to targeted areas and groups, needs assessment can be used systematically to reassess community needs for comparison with baseline data. The difference indicates the magnitude of impact specific interventions have had on reducing identified needs.

The community advisory committees review and analyze reassessment data about targeted problems and groups, using this data to replan for future interventions. By evaluating their plans, the advisory committees are able to recommend changes to the planning committees; these, in turn, recommend to the board of directors new plans and changes in the allocation of staff efforts and financial resources.

## SUMMARY

Needs assessment data can be used to facilitate planning and evaluation at many levels of complex human service delivery systems. The Community Impact Planning Model is a strategy for planning and evaluating human services which emphasizes consumer participation in developing service plans. Members of the community, key informants, consumers, and potential consumers are able to help identify the community's needs and work with members of the board, management staff, and service deliverers to plan service interventions, evaluate their effectiveness, reassess needs, and replan services.

Through community involvement and interagency coordination in planning, the effectiveness of a local human service delivery system is maximized, and services are directed toward the elimination of community need and the enhancement of living skills.

## NOTE

1. See the Community Mental Health Center Amendments, Public Law 94-63, Section 304 (b), Title III, 1975. See also Title XX of the Social Security Act, Public Law 93-746, 1974 and Amendments to Title XX of the Social Security Act, Public Law 94-401, Sections 228.28 (a), 228.31, and 228.32, 1976.

# SAMPLE INSTRUMENTS

INSTRUMENT 1

GENERAL PUBLIC

Interviewer:_____

Date of Interview: _____

Time of Day: _____

Length of Interview
(in minutes): _____

Sample Area:_____

1. Location of interview?                          Col. 1: _____

---

|  | City | Town | Rural (Be specific) | Township |

2. (If not self-evident, ask:)

   What type of house do you live in?                    2: _____

   ☐ Single family dwelling *(1)*
   ☐ Duplex *(2)*
   ☐ Apartment *(3)*
   ☐ Mobile home *(4)*
   ☐ Other (specify) _____ *(5)*

3. How long have you lived at your current address?       3: _____

   ☐ Under 1 year *(1)*        ☐ 10-14 years *(4)*
   ☐ 1-4 years *(2)*          ☐ Over 15 years *(5)*
   ☐ 5-9 years *(3)*          ☐ Refused *(6)*

4. How long have you lived in [specify county]?           4: _____

   ☐ Under 1 year *(1)*        ☐ 10-14 years *(4)*
   ☐ 1-4 years *(2)*          ☐ Over 15 years *(5)*
   ☐ 5-9 years *(3)*          ☐ Refused *(6)*

5. Race                                              5: _____

   ☐ white *(1)*
   ☐ black *(2)*
   ☐ Other (specify)_____ *(3)*

6.  Sex                                                          Col. 6: _____

    ☐ male *(1)*
    ☐ female *(2)*

7.  What is your age?                                            7: _____

    ☐ Under 25 *(1)*      ☐ 45-54 years *(4)*
    ☐ 25-34 years *(2)*    ☐ Over 54 years *(5)*
    ☐ 35-44 years *(3)*

8.  How many children in the following age groups presently live in this household?

    Under 5 years old _____                 8: _____

    5-10 years _____                    9: _____

    11-15 years _____                  10: _____

    16-18 years _____                  11: _____

    None _____ *(1)*                 12: _____

9.  How many adults age 19 and older live in this household?
    (include respondent)                                        13: _____

    Number _____ ( # )

    Refused _____ *(0)*

10. What is your marital status?                                 14: _____

    ☐ Single *(1)*      ☐ Separated *(4)*
    ☐ Married *(2)*    ☐ Divorced *(5)*
    ☐ Widowed *(3)*    ☐ Refused *(6)*

11. What is the highest level of education you have completed?    15: _____

    ☐ Grade school *(1)*      ☐ College graduate *(4)*
    ☐ High school graduate or GED  ☐ Other (specify) *(5)*
    *(2)*                        _____
    ☐ Attended college *(3)*    ☐ Refused *(6)*

12. What is your job or occupation? (Be specific)                Col. 16: _____

_____

    (If a specific occupation is given, do not check the responses below.)

    ☐ None *(1)*
    ☐ Housewife *(2)*
    ☐ Student *(3)*
    ☐ Retired *(4)*
    ☐ No Response *(5)*

13. Are you presently employed? 17: _____

    ☐ Yes *(1)*
    ☐ No *(2)*
    ☐ No Response *(3)*

14. Do you have a religious preference? 18: _____

    ☐ Yes* *(1)*
    ☐ No *(2)*

    *If yes, what denomination? _____
    (Example, Catholic, Lutheran, etc.)

15. All neighborhoods have problems. In your opinion, what are three
    problems in your neighborhood? 19: _____

    1) _____
    2) _____
    3) _____
    ☐ Don't Know *(1)*
    ☐ No Response *(2)*

16. All communities have problems. In your opinion, what are three
    problems in your community? Col. 20: _____

    1) _____
    2) _____
    3) _____
    ☐ Don't Know *(1)*
    ☐ No Response *(2)*

17. All schools have problems. In your opinion, what are three
    problems in your schools? Col. 21: _____

    1) _____
    2) _____
    3) _____
    ☐ Don't Know *(1)*
    ☐ No Response *(2)*

18. All people face problems in their daily lives. In the past five
    years, what are some of the problems of living you have faced? 22: _____

    _____
    _____
    _____
    ☐ Don't Know *(1)*      ☐ No Response *(2)*

19. Other than family or friends, if you had a serious personal or
    family problem, who would you go to first for help?                23: _____

    _____

    ☐ Don't Know *(1)*          ☐ No Response *(2)*

20. Would you seek help with a personal or family problem
    from a counseling agency?                                 Col. 24: _____

    ☐ Yes *(1)*                 ☐ No *(2)*

    If no, why wouldn't you _____

    _____

21. From the list of problems, choose the three (3) that you think are the most
    serious in your community. (Give list to person being interviewed.)

    ☐ Marital Conflict *(01)*
    ☐ Rape *(02)*
    ☐ Racial Conflict *(03)*                           25-26: _____
    ☐ Venereal Disease *(04)*
    ☐ Mental Retardation *(05)*                        27-28: _____
    ☐ Physically Handicapped *(06)*
    ☐ Problems of Raising Children *(07)*              29-30: _____
    ☐ Family Conflict *(08)*
    ☐ Unemployment *(09)*
    ☐ Child Abuse *(10)*
    ☐ Alcoholism *(11)*
    ☐ Juvenile Delinquency *(12)*
    ☐ Poverty *(13)*
    ☐ Drug Abuse *(14)*
    ☐ Crime *(15)*
    ☐ School Problems *(16)*
    ☐ Problems of Senior Citizens *(17)*
    ☐ Other Problems (specify) *(18)*  _____
    ☐ No Response *(99)*                               31-32: _____

22. What factors, if any, would keep you from seeking help
    from a mental health center or similar helping agency?
    (Give respondent list.)

    ☐ It wouldn't help *(1)*                           Col. 33: _____
    ☐ Lack of transportation *(1)*                         34: _____
    ☐ Agency usually not open when help is needed *(1)*     35: _____
    ☐ Fear of what others might think *(1)*                36: _____
    ☐ Cost of services *(1)*                               37: _____
    ☐ Location of agency *(1)*                             38: _____
    ☐ Don't know where they are *(1)*                      39: _____
    ☐ Other (specify) _____ *(1)*        40: _____
    ☐ None *(8)*                                           41: _____
    ☐ No response *(9)*

23. What are the two most effective ways to inform you about
    services provided by agencies in your community?

    ☐ Television *(1)*
    ☐ Word of Mouth *(2)*
    ☐ Radio *(3)*
    ☐ Educational Talks *(4)*                                    42: _____
    ☐ Pamphlet *(5)*
    ☐ Local Newspaper *(6)*                                      43: _____
    ☐ Other (specify) _____ *(7)*
    ☐ Don't Know *(8)*
    ☐ No Response *(9)*

24. Do you know of the following agencies?

    |                      | YES | NO |  |
    |----------------------|-----|-----|-----|
    |                      | ☐ *(1)* | ☐ *(2)* | Col. 44: _____ |
    | [List key human      | ☐ *(1)* | ☐ *(2)* | 45: _____ |
    | services agencies    | ☐ *(1)* | ☐ *(2)* | 46: _____ |
    | providing services   | ☐ *(1)* | ☐ *(2)* | 47: _____ |
    | to geographic        | ☐ *(1)* | ☐ *(2)* | 48: _____ |
    | area sampled.]       | ☐ *(1)* | ☐ *(2)* | 49: _____ |

25. The above agencies provide the following services. Select three
    that you would like to see expanded. (Give list to respondent).

    ☐ Help with family problems *(01)*
    ☐ Parent education *(02)*
    ☐ Counseling with children *(03)*                           50-51: _____
    ☐ Alcohol education *(04)*
    ☐ Assertiveness training *(05)*
    ☐ Drug abuse counseling *(06)*                              52-53: _____
    ☐ Suicide prevention *(07)*
    ☐ Drug education *(08)*
    ☐ Marital counseling *(09)*                                 54-55: _____
    ☐ Alcohol abuse counseling *(10)*
    ☐ Counseling with adults *(11)*
    ☐ Don't know *(98)*                                         56-57: _____
    ☐ Refused *(99)*

26. There are a number of services available to help people
    with problems of living. What additional services do you
    think are needed in your community?

    _____

    _____

    ☐ Have enough services *(1)*                                Col. 58: _____
    ☐ Don't Know *(8)*                                          59: _____
    ☐ No Response *(9)*                                         60: _____

27. The following is a list of proposed services. Indicate those
services you would like to see developed in the next three
years. (Give list to respondent.)

| YES | NO | | |
|-----|-----|-----|-----|
| ☐ (1) | ☐ (2) | Parent education services available in the community | 61: _____ |
| ☐ (1) | ☐ (2) | Mental health services provided closer to where you live | 62: _____ |
| ☐ (1) | ☐ (2) | Residential center for adolescents with alcohol and drug problems | 63: _____ |
| ☐ (1) | ☐ (2) | Residential center for adolescents with emotional problems | 64: _____ |
| ☐ (1) | ☐ (2) | Drug education seminars for parents. | 65: _____ |

☐ No Response (9)                                                                   66: _____

28. Would you select the income category which approximates
your family income? (Give respondent Income Category
Card.)

☐ Income Category (from Income Card)  (   )          67-68: _____
☐ Refused (8)                                                             69: _____
☐ Didn't know (9)                                                        70: _____

Group #                                                              Col. 75-76:  _____

| | |
|---|---|
| General Public | (01) |
| Bartenders | (02) |
| School Administrators | (03) |
| School Counselors | (04) |
| School Teachers | (05) |
| Law Enforcement Officers | (06) |
| Nurses | (07) |
| Clergy | (08) |
| Medical Doctors | (09) |
| Lawyers | (10) |
| Agency Personnel and Administrators | (11) |

Subject #                                                            Col. 77-80:  _____

## INCOME CATEGORIES
(for use with Item 28, Instrument 1)

| | Yearly Income | Monthly Income | Weekly Income |
|---|---|---|---|
| 1. | Under $2,000 | Under $166 | Under $38 |
| 2. | $2,000 – $3,999 | $166 – $333 | $38 – $77 |
| 3. | $4,000 – $5,999 | $344 – $500 | $78 – $115 |
| 4. | $6,000 – $7,999 | $501 – $667 | $116 – $154 |
| 5. | $8,000 – $9,999 | $668 – $833 | $155 – $192 |
| 6. | $10,000 – $11,999 | $834 – $999 | $193 – $230 |
| 7. | $12,000 – $13,999 | $1,000 – $1,167 | $231 – $269 |
| 8. | $14,000 – $15,999 | $1,168 – $1,333 | $270 – $307 |
| 9. | $16,000 – $17,999 | $1,334 – $1,499 | $308 – $346 |
| 10. | $18,000 – $19,999 | $1,500 – $1,666 | $347 – $384 |
| 11. | $20,000 – $24,999 | $1,667 – $2,083 | $385 – $480 |
| 12. | $25,000 – $29,999 | $2,084 – $2,449 | $481 – $576 |
| 13. | $30,000 – Over | $2,450 – Over | $577 – Over |

INSTRUMENT 2

## KEY INFORMANT

Date Questionnaire Completed _____

1. In what city/town is your agency located?      Col. 1: _____

2. Does your agency serve all of [specified county]?      2: _____

   ☐ Yes *(1)*
   ☐ No *(2)*

3. What is your position or title?      3: _____

Are you an administrator?

   ☐ Yes *(1)*
   ☐ No *(2)*

4.  How long have you lived in [specified county]?                        4: _____

☐ Under 1 year *(1)*          ☐ 10-14 years *(4)*
☐ 1-4 years *(2)*             ☐ Over 15 years *(5)*
☐ 5-9 years *(3)*             ☐ Not Applicable *(6)*

5.  Race                                                                   5: _____

☐ White *(1)*
☐ Black *(2)*
☐ Other (specify) _____*(3)*

6.  Sex

☐ Male *(1)*
☐ Female *(2)*

7.  What is your age?                                                      7: _____

☐ Under 25 years *(1)*        ☐ 45-54 years *(4)*
☐ 25-34 years *(2)*           ☐ 55-64 years *(5)*
☐ 35-44 years *(3)*           ☐ Over 64 years *(6)*

8.  How long have you worked for your agency?               Col. 8: _____

☐ Under 1 year *(1)*          ☐ 11-15 years *(4)*
☐ 1-5 years *(2)*             ☐ 16 years or over *(5)*
☐ 6-10 years *(3)*

9.  Marital Status                                                        14: _____

☐ Married *(1)*               ☐ Divorced *(4)*
☐ Single *(2)*                ☐ Separated *(5)*
☐ Widowed *(3)*

10. Check educational background                                          15:_____

☐ High school graduate *(2)*      ☐ Attended graduate school *(7)*
☐ Attended college *(3)*          ☐ Graduate degree (specify)
☐ College graduate *(4)*
                                  _____ *(8)*

11. All neighborhoods have problems. In your opinion, what are three
    problems in your neighborhood?

    1) _____
    2) _____
    3) _____

12. All communities have problems. In your opinion, what are three problems in your community?

   1) _____

   2) _____

   3) _____

13. All schools have problems. In your opinion, what are three problems in your schools?

   1) _____

   2) _____

   3) _____

14. All people face problems in their daily lives. In the past five years, what are some of the problems of living you have faced?

   _____

   _____

   _____

   _____

15. From the list of problems, choose the *three* (3) that you think are the most serious in your community. (Please check.)

   ☐ Marital Conflict *(01)*
   ☐ Rape *(02)*
   ☐ Racial Conflict *(03)*             Col. 25-26: _____
   ☐ Venereal Disease *(04)*
   ☐ Mental Retardation *(05)*          27-28: _____
   ☐ Physically Handicapped *(06)*
   ☐ Problems of Raising Children *(07)*  29-30: _____
   ☐ Family Conflict *(08)*
   ☐ Unemployment *(09)*
   ☐ Child Abuse *(10)*
   ☐ Alcoholism *(11)*
   ☐ Juvenile Delinquency *(12)*
   ☐ Poverty *(13)*
   ☐ Drug Abuse *(14)*
   ☐ Crime *(15)*
   ☐ School Problems *(16)*
   ☐ Problems of Senior Citizens *(17)*
   ☐ Other Problems (specify) *(18)*  _____

   _____

   _____

16. What kinds of mental health or related problems do you encounter
    most frequently in persons using your services?

    _____
    _____
    _____

17. Question 16 identifies problems you frequently encounter in your
    work. In which of these areas do you feel training would enhance
    your effectiveness?

    _____
    _____
    _____
    _____

18. Do you feel there are adequate resources within your        Col. 31: _____
    agency to deal with these problems? (Question 16)

    ☐ Yes *(1)*
    ☐ No *(2)*

    Please elaborate on your response. _____
    _____

19. Do you feel there are adequate community resources              32: _____
    available when you need to refer?

    ☐ Yes *(1)*
    ☐ No *(2)*

    Please elaborate on your response. _____
    _____

20. What factors, if any, do you feel would keep people from
    seeking help from a mental health center or similar helping
    agency? (Please check.)

    ☐ It wouldn't help *(1)*                                    33: _____
    ☐ Lack of transportation *(1)*                             34: _____
    ☐ Agency usually not open when help is needed *(1)*        35: _____
    ☐ Fear of what others might think *(1)*                    36: _____
    ☐ Cost of services *(1)*                                   37: _____
    ☐ Location of agency *(1)*                                 38: _____
    ☐ Don't know where they are *(1)*                          39: _____
    ☐ Other (specify) ( )                                      40: _____
    ☐ None ( )                                                 41: _____

21. What are the two (2) most effective ways to inform you
    about services provided by agencies in your community?
    (Check only two)      42: _____

    ☐ Television *(1)*      ☐ Pamphlet *(5)*      43: _____
    ☐ Word of Mouth *(2)*      ☐ Local newspaper *(6)*
    ☐ Radio *(3)*      ☐ Other (specify) *(7)*
    ☐ Educational Talks *(4)*

22. In what ways does your agency inform the public about its services?
    _____
    _____
    _____

23. Do you know of the following agencies?
    [List key human service agencies providing
    services to geographic area sampled.]

         ☐ *(1)*    ☐ *(2)*      44: _____
         ☐ *(1)*    ☐ *(2)*      45: _____
         ☐ *(1)*    ☐ *(2)*      46: _____
         ☐ *(1)*    ☐ *(2)*      47: _____
         ☐ *(1)*    ☐ *(2)*      48: _____
         ☐ *(1)*    ☐ *(2)*      49: _____

24. The above agencies provide the following services. Select
    *three* (3) that you would like to see expanded.

    ☐ Help with Family Problems *(01)*
    ☐ Parent Education *(02)*
    ☐ Counseling with Children *(03)*      Col. 50-51: _____
    ☐ Alcohol Education *(04)*
    ☐ Assertiveness Training *(05)*      52-53: _____
    ☐ Drug Abuse Counseling *(06)*
    ☐ Suicide Prevention *(07)*      54-55: _____
    ☐ Drug Education *(08)*
    ☐ Marital Counseling *(09)*
    ☐ Alcohol Abuse Counseling *(10)*
    ☐ Counseling with Adults *(11)*

25. How often have you referred people to a mental
    health agency?      Col. 56: _____

    ☐ Never *(1)*
    ☐ Less than 3 times per year *(2)*
    ☐ 3-6 times per year *(3)*
    ☐ 7-10 times per year *(4)*
    ☐ More than 10 times per year *(5)*

26. Is there a need for more emergency mental health
    and related services?                                        57: _____

    ☐ Yes *(1)*
    ☐ No *(2)*

    Please elaborate on your response. _____
    _____

27. There are a number of services available to help people with
    problems of living. What additional services do you think are
    needed in your community?
    _____
    _____
    _____

    ☐ Have enough services *(1)*                                 58: _____

28. Do you encounter problems making a referral to other
    agencies?                                                    59: _____

    ☐ Yes *(1)*
    ☐ No *(2)*

    Please elaborate on your response. _____
    _____

29. Is it clear to you what agencies will handle what
    problems?                                               Col. 60: _____

    ☐ Yes *(1)*
    ☐ No *(2)*

    Please elaborate on your response. _____
    _____

30. The following is a list of proposed services. Indicate those
    services you would like to see developed in the next three years.

    ☐ Yes *(1)*    ☐ No *(2)*    Parent education services
                                 available in the community      61: _____

    ☐ Yes *(1)*    ☐ No *(2)*    Mental health services
                                 provided closer to where
                                 you live                        62: _____

    ☐ Yes *(1)*    ☐ No *(2)*    Residential center for
                                 adolescents with alcohol
                                 and drug problems               63: _____

    ☐ Yes *(1)*    ☐ No *(2)*    Residential center for
                                 adolescents with emotional
                                 problems                        64: _____

    ☐ Yes *(1)*    ☐ No *(1)*    Drug education seminars
                                 for parents                     65: _____

31. How could cooperation between you and a mental health agency be improved (Be specific)

_____

_____

_____

_____

32. Which of the following areas would improve cooperation between you and a mental health agency?

☐ Information about type of services available *(1)*          Col. 67: _____
☐ A contact person in the agency to assist you in
    making referrals *(2)*                                                     68: _____
☐ Information about fees, intake procedures,
    confidentiality, etc. *(3)*                                                69: _____
☐ Joint skill development workshops *(4)*                          70: _____
☐ Additional areas (Be specific) *(5)*                               71: _____

_____

_____

_____

33. With which *two* (2) of the following do you work
    *most frequently*?                                                       72: _____

☐ Clergy *(1)*                                                                 73: _____
☐ Nurses *(2)*
☐ Law Enforcement *(3)*
☐ School Personnel *(4)*
☐ Lawyers *(5)*
☐ Medical Doctors *(6)*
☐ Psychiatrists *(7)*
☐ Social Agencies (Please specify) *(8)*

_____

34. What response would you like to have following a
    referral to a mental health agency?                          Col. 74: _____

☐ Letter of Acknowledgement *(1)*
☐ Follow-up Telephone Call *(2)*
☐ Face-to-Face Consultation *(3)*
☐ No Response *(4)*
☐ Other *(5)*

_____

# APPENDIX B

# SAMPLE PRESS RELEASES

## INITIAL PRESS RELEASE

(printed on agency letterhead)

(date)

The staffs and boards of directors of two local human service agencies are undertaking a survey project to better understand the service needs of residents in [geographic area]. The [agency(s) name(s) and location(s)] have begun the ambitious project of obtaining information pertaining to how the community member perceives mental health needs.

Mental health needs refer to those personal factors and situations which determine how effective and happy we are in our daily lives. All people face problems in living, and generally we are able to find a resolution to these problems. When life problems become greater than our ability to solve them, often we look to human service agencies for help. In order for these agencies to be most effective in helping people, the agencies must be prepared to offer the kinds of assistance which persons of that community need.

In an effort to obtain information on what individual consumers believe their needs to be, the [agency(s) name(s) and location(s)] will be conducting a door-to-door interview survey with the residents of [geographic parameters]. Volunteers working in teams will be knocking on the doors of approximately [specify number] residents to ask questions pertaining to human service needs. Surveying will begin [specify date] and continue through [specify date]. Interviewers will be properly identified for the protection of all concerned.

In addition to door-to-door interviews, questionnaires will be mailed to persons in the community who work in the human service professions. [list all key informants] will be surveyed.

Your cooperation in this effort to improve mental health is greatly appreciated.

## FOLLOW-UP PRESS RELEASE

On [specify day and date] individuals from the local community will be participating in a mental health needs assessment survey.

The survey is being conducted by the [agency(s) name(s) and location(s)].

Approximately [specify number] interviews will be administered to residents living in [geographic area] for the purpose of better understanding individual and community human service needs.

The information gathered will be used for planning programs to improve delivery of mental health and related human services. To ensure success of this project, the cooperation of individuals contacted in the community is extremely important.

Interviewers conducting the door-to-door interviews will have: (1) pictured identification badges; and (2) letters identifying their participation in the project. The legitimacy of each interviewer can be verified by calling your local police department.

The human service needs assessment survey is a major step toward involving the individual living in the community in the planning of services partially supported by public tax money.

If you are contacted, please take a few minutes of your time to get involved in shaping mental health service delivery in your community.

If you have any questions regarding the survey, contact [name and telephone number of principal investigator].

## PUBLIC SERVICE ANNOUNCEMENT: RADIO

The _____will be conducting a sur-
                    agency(s) name(s)
vey on _____ in _____. This public opinion
            (date)                (geographic location)
survey will provide consumers with an opportunity to express their concerns and needs for developing local human services. If contacted, please take this opportunity to make your opinions known. The success of human service planning is dependent on the participation of you, the consumer. Interviewers will be properly identified. Thank you.

# APPENDIX C

# SAMPLE CONSENT FORM

## CONSENT FORM

1. I acknowledge that I have willingly participated in this survey.

2. I have been informed of my right not to answer any question(s) asked by the interviewer.

3. I understand that the results of this survey will be used in planning for mental health service delivery to this area.

4. I permit the researcher to use the information I have provided, with the understanding that the researcher will take all necessary precautions to ensure my anonymity.

_____

Signature

_____

Date

# APPENDIX D

# SAMPLE LETTER TO CONSUMER AND KEY INFORMANT PARTICIPANTS

## LETTER OF INTRODUCTION

(printed on agency letterhead)

[date]

To Whom It May Concern:

This is to certify that the bearer of this letter, when wearing an official Community Oriented Needs Assessment name tag with picture, is authorized to conduct interviews of the general public in our behalf.

The intent of this interview is to determine what you feel are the problems and needs of people in [geographic area]. Your cooperation is greatly appreciated.

If you desire further verification of the bearer of this letter, please call your local police department or:

[    investigating agency(s) name(s)    ]
[    address                            ]
[    telephone number                   ]

Thank you again.

Sincerely,

BOARD OF DIRECTORS


John R. Smith
President

## LETTER TO KEY INFORMANTS

(printed on agency letterhead)

[date]


In order to plan for and deliver more effective human services in this area, we are conducting a survey of [geographic area]. In addition to interviewing a sample of the general public, questionnaires are being forwarded to individuals who provide human services within this area.

The information generated by this undertaking will shape the future of mental health and other human service programming in [geographic area].

Your assistance in completing the enclosed questionnaire is greatly appreciated. Please return the questionnaire, using the prepaid envelope, at your earliest convenience.

YOUR PERSONAL COOPERATION IS IMPERATIVE TO THE OVERALL SUCCESS OF THIS ENDEAVOR.

Thank you again.

Sincerely,

BOARD OF DIRECTORS


John R. Smith
President

# APPENDIX E

# EXAMPLES OF DATA SOURCES

## DATA SOURCES

*United States Census of Population*

Population variables: age, sex, race, density, percentage urban, persons per household

Housing patterns: total units, owned units, rental units, type of dwelling, average number of persons per unit, length of residence

Income characteristics

Educational information

Employment characteristics: size of labor force, sex differences, unemployment rate, occupation distribution

Data on aged: age range distributions, sex, race, marital status, living environment, housing patterns, income, employment rates

*Law Enforcement Records*

Crime Index Offenses: homicide, forcible rape, robbery, battery, burglary, theft, and so on

Other offenses: vandalism, sex offenses, arson, disorderly conduct, drug/alcohol related offenses, and so on

Crimes per sworn officer

Commitments to correctional institutions

Juvenile crime rate

*Public Health Records*

Infant death rates

Suicides

Number of registered physicians/nurses

Number of long-term care beds

Venereal disease statistics

Abortion rates

*Public Assistance Records*

Divorce rates

Number receiving assistance for: child care, old age, blindness, general assistance, and so on

*Education Records*

Drop-out rates

Suspension rates

Population of schools: sex, age, race, and so on
Public school pupils per teacher

*Mental Health Records*

Population: age, sex, race, marital status, income, geographic residence, diagnosis,
and so on

# APPENDIX F

# EXAMPLE OF SAMPLING PROCEDURE

## SAMPLING PROCEDURE*

The area of interest has a population age 18 and older of 5000. A sample size of 100 is desired.

Step 1: Computation of Sampling Fraction

$$f = \frac{n}{(N)\ (CR)\ (RR)\ (OR)}$$

where n = sample size
      N = population size
     CR = coverage rate (.95)
     RR = response (.75)
     OR = occupancy rate (.98)

$$f = \frac{100}{(5000)\ (.95)\ (.75)\ (.98)}$$

$$= \frac{100}{3491.25}$$

$$f = .028643$$

or

$$f = \frac{1}{.028643}$$

$$f = 34.91 \text{ or } 35$$

Thus every 35th housing unit is used to select the final "chunks."

Step 2: Computation of Adjusted Number of Interviews

$$n' = N/f$$

$$= 5000/35$$

$$n' = 142.86 \text{ or } 143$$

Thus 143 interviews must be attempted in order to complete approximately 100.

Step 3: Stratification, Chunking, and Application of Sampling Fraction

The area can be stratified into five strata based on race, economic factors, and a rural-urban dimension. Following is a listing of "chunks" and the number of housing units in each "chunk" for the rural stratum.

| Chunk Number | Number of Housing Units |
|:---:|:---:|
| 1 | 13 |
| 2* | 18 |
| 3 | 17 |
| 4 | 12 |
| 5* | 20 |
| 6 | 12 |
| 7 | 12 |
| 8* | 13 |
| 9 | 16 |
| 10 | 15 |
| 11* | 14 |
| 12 | 13 |
| 13 | 20 |
| 14* | 19 |
| 15 | 12 |
| 16 | 14 |
| 17* | 15 |
| 18 | 17 |
| 19* | 19 |
| 20 | 18 |
| 21 | 12 |
| 22* | 12 |

Starting with a randomly chosen number between 1 and 35 (e.g., 23) and counting the housing units, the first "chunk" selected is number 2. Starting with "chunk" number 3, and counting to the 35th housing unit yields number 5 as the second selected "chunk." This procedure is continued through stratum. The selected "chunks" are indicated by asterisks. Thus "chunks" are selected from the rural stratum. This same procedure is followed for the remaining four strata.

Step 4: Checking Selected Chunks

The selected "chunks" in all strata are checked in the field, and necessary additions and deletions of housing units are made.

Step 5: Selection of Housing Units

A total of 51 chunks are selected from all five strata. The number of housing units to be selected from each "chunk" is given by:

$$\text{Number of Housing Units} = \frac{n'}{\text{Number of Selected Chunks}}$$

$$= \frac{143}{51}$$

Number of Housing Units = 2.80 or 3

Thus 3 housing units must be randomly chosen from each of the selected "chunks." To do this in the first "chunk" of the rural stratum the housing units are numbered 1 to 17 and a random number table is consulted. The first number in the random number table less than or equal to 17 is 15. Housing Unit Number 15 is chosen. The second and third numbers are 3 and 7. Thus Housing Units 3, 7, and 15 are selected for interviewing from this "chunk." This procedure is then followed for the remaining selected "chunks" in the rural stratum and in the other four strata.

The end result is that 153 specific housing units are identified for interviewing. This is slightly more than the required n' = 143 because of the rounding up in Step 5.

*For the sake of clarity and brevity, the numbers used in the example are unrealistically small.

# EXAMPLE OF DATA USE FOR SERVICE DELIVERY

## DATA USE

The following is taken from a report based on actual use of needs assessment data. It is illustrative of how the various types of data can be used to identify problem areas and suggest approaches to the solution of these problems. This report was constructed to provide information on potential mental health service needs of children and adolescents in the catchment area.

## IDENTIFYING ISSUES OF CONCERN

Problem identification can be approached from numerous directions. One means is the identification of populations at risk, i.e., populations where the probable need for human services is great.

Demographic age data (Table 1) indicates that 13.6% of clients with open cases at the mental health center are between the ages of 13 and 17. For the entire county, adolescents between 13 and 17 comprise approximately 10% of the total population. This difference of 3.6% indicates that the adolescent population consumes mental

TABLE 1 Demographic Information
Relating to Children and Adolescents

*U.S. Census Tract Data, 1970*

| Age Range | Percentage of County Population |
|---|---|
| Under 5 years | 8.5 |
| 5-9 years | 10.2 |
| 10-14 years | 10.7 |
| 15-19 years | 9.1 |

13-17 years = 9.95%

*CONA Data*

| Age Range | Percentage of Total Open Cases |
|---|---|
| 0-5 years | 3.8 |
| 6-12 years | 8.5 |
| 13-17 years | 13.6 |

health services beyond what might be considered average per capita total population for this age range. There are many possible reasons for this difference. However, generally it is accepted that the teen-age years are confounded by problems associated with identity development, peer acceptance, acceptance of responsibility, struggles to obtain independence and life-goal decision-making.

Family problems and divorce rates (Table 2) impact on the stability of youth environments and serve to create a population of children, adolescents, and families who may need services to resolve life problems.

Table 3 illustrates how certain key informant groups and general public respondents view their concern over specific community problems which directly affect the

TABLE 2   Family Problems and Divorce Rates*

| Issues of Human Concern | Percentage of County Population | Percentage of State Population |
|---|---|---|
| Aid to Dependent Children Recipients | 4.92 | 3.3 |
| Divorces | 3.95 | 2.69 |
| Juveniles Institutionalized for Crimes | .03 | .05 |

*Information obtained from public records

TABLE 3   Perceived Problems of the Community

| Problems Relating To | Ranking | |
|---|---|---|
| | Key Informant | General Public |
| Raising Children | 1 (42.0%) | 4 (25.5%) |
| Juvenile Delinquency | 5 (27.4%) | 3 (26.5%) |
| School Problems | 9 (17.9%) | 8 (16.5%) |
| Family Conflict | 3 (35.5%) | 10 (09.5%) |

Rankings of Perceived Problems by Group

| Group | Raising Children | Juvenile Delinquency | School Problems | Family Conflict |
|---|---|---|---|---|
| School Administrators | 1 | 5 | 7 | 2 |
| School Counselors | 1 | 7 | 3 | 1 |
| School Teachers | 1 | 3 | 5 | 2 |
| Law Enforcement | 3 | 1 | 9 | 4 |
| Nurses | 3 | 6 | 10 | 5 |
| Clergy | 3 | 6 | 6 | 2 |
| Medical Doctors | 5 | 9 | 5 | 1 |
| Lawyers | 2 | 3 | 9 | 3 |
| Social Agency | 2 | 10 | 8 | 2 |

lives of children and adolescents. Of 18 possible community problems, the results indicate principal concerns about childrearing and juvenile delinquency.

Key informants and general public respondents differ substantially on the importance placed on family conflict as a community problem.

In reviewing the responses to community problems, the reader is advised to observe differences in how different key informant groups respond to problems affecting youth. For example, with regard to juvenile delinquency, those persons who as professionals are more likely to encounter juveniles in delinquent behavior are those indicating juvenile delinquency as a major concern.

One item not listed on Table 3 which emerges as a major concern is substance abuse. Substance abuse is a problem which certainly affects the lives of youth. However, the nature of the information available from the needs assessment does not allow for determination of the particular age range for which the concern arises.

The above information can be summarized as indicating that adolescents are a risk group, potentially in need of human services, due to the community problems and personal growth issues they experience as part of their development.

One issue, therefore, is the adequacy of available services for helping adolescents deal with life stress.

## TREATMENT PREFERENCES

Key informants and general public respondents were asked to indicate which services they would like to see expanded when given a list of eleven alternatives. Table 4 represents how respondent groups reacted to services directly related to problems experienced by children and adolescents.

For key informants, a definite preference was indicated for additional services which would help with family problems; 64% of all key informants indicated this alternative as a preference. Key informants favor expanding youth counseling services as a second preference, although they express this less frequently.

General public respondents also indicated a preference for expanding services to help with family problems and youth problems. There appears to be little variation between geographic areas with regard to the general public's degree of interest in expanding youth-oriented helping services.

The general public respondents' highest preference, expanding drug abuse counseling, is not indicated on Table 4. The reason for not including these results is that the degree, if any, to which expansion relates to services for youth cannot be determined.

## REACTIONS TO RESIDENTIAL TYPES OF TREATMENT

Key informant responses to an open-ended question on what additional services are needed in the community indicated some preference for a helping center for

TABLE 4    Services Respondents Would Like To See
Expanded

| Service | Ranking | |
|---------|---------|---|
| | Key Informant | General Public |
| Help with Family Problems | 1 (64.6%) | 2 (36.9%) |
| Counseling with Children | 2 (40.5%) | 3 (33.0%) |

Rankings of Services by Group

| Group | Help with Family Problems | Counseling with Children |
|-------|---------------------------|--------------------------|
| General Public Stratum 1 | 3 (35.1%) | 2 (37.2%) |
| General Public Stratum 2 | 2 (40.0%) | 3 (32.6%) |
| General Public Stratum 3 | 4 (33.1%) | 3 (34.0%) |
| General Public Stratum 4 | 1 (36.9%) | 4 (29.8%) |
| General Public Stratum 5 | 1 (40.5%) | 4 (28.6%) |
| School Administrators | 1 (80.7%) | 4 (31.6%) |
| School Counselors | 1 (83.3%) | 3 (36.7%) |
| School Teachers | 1 (65.7%) | 2 (56.6%) |
| Law Enforcement | 1 (72.7%) | 2 (37.3%) |
| Nurses | 1 (45.5%) | 2 (40.9%) |
| Clergy | 1 (81.1%) | 3 (35.1%) |
| Medical Doctors | 1 (44.4%) | 1 (44.4%) |
| Lawyers | 1 (64.7%) | 2 (35.3%) |
| Social Agency | 1 (56.0%) | 3 (33.3%) |

TABLE 5    Examples of Open-Ended Responses to
Additional Services Needed

| Residential Types of Treatment | Key Informant Group | Number of Respondent |
|--------------------------------|---------------------|----------------------|
| Center to Help Adolescents (Juveniles) at High Risk | Clergy | 3 |
| | Teachers | 3 |
| | Law Enforcement | 3 |
| Halfway House/Runaway Center | Lawyers | 1 |
| | Nurses | 1 |
| Help for Young People with Problems at Home | Clergy | 1 |
| | Teachers | 1 |
| | Law Enforcement | 3 |
| Better Child Care Facilities | Nurses | 1 |

TABLE 6    Reactions to Proposed Residential Treatment*

*For Adolescents with Alcohol and Drug Problems:*

| Total Response | Key Informants | General Public |
|---|---|---|
| Yes | 63.2% | 71.2% |
| No | 7.7% | 15.5% |
| Difference (Yes/No) | 55.5% | 55.7% |
| No Opinion | 29.1% | 13.3% |

*For Adolescents with Emotional Problems:*

| Total Response | Key Informants | General Public |
|---|---|---|
| Yes | 67.9% | 70.1% |
| No | 7.4% | 14.6% |
| Difference (Yes/No) | 60.5% | 55.5% |
| No Opinion | 25.0% | 15.3% |

*Figures indicate percentage of total sample giving identified response to item.

youth (Table 5). Of 17 responses indicating a need to expand youth helping services, 12 indicated the need for some type of youth helping center.

All respondents were asked to express their opinion about residential helping centers as a helping modality for adolescents experiencing (1) alcohol/drug problems and (2) emotional problems.

Key informants and general public respondents strongly favored both proposed residential programs. Opposition was greater among general public respondents than key informants; however, the overall result of those in favor (minus those opposed) was basically equivalent for key informants and general public respondents (See Table 6).

Analysis by key informant groups (Table 7) reveals that law enforcement personnel, social agency personnel, and nurses are the groups most in favor of residential placement for adolescents with alcohol and drug problems. School personnel and social agency personnel are the groups most actively supporting residential placement for adolescents with emotional problems. Of the key informant groups, law enforcement personnel are least in favor of residential placement for adolescents with emotional problems.

Table 8 provides a geographical breakdown of how key informants and general public respondents responded to the question of residential treatment for adolescents.

General public support of residential treatment for adolescents appears to be strongly supported in geographic areas other than stratum 4 and stratum 5, the rural area. The strongest opposition to residential treatment appears to occur in stratum 4.

TABLE 7   Reactions by Key Informant Group to
Proposed Residential Treatment for Adolescents

| Key Informant Group | Alcohol & Drug Problems | Emotional Problems |
|---|---|---|
| School Personnel (Teachers, Counselors, Administrators — 184) | | |
| Yes | 59.6% | 74.2% |
| No | 7.0% | 6.4% |
| Difference (Yes/No) | 52.6% | 67.8% |
| No Opinion | 33.4% | 19.0% |
| Law Enforcement (65) | | |
| Yes | 71.6% | 55.2% |
| No | 10.5% | 13.4% |
| Difference (Yes/No) | 61.1% | 41.8% |
| No Opinion | 17.9% | 31.3% |
| Nurses (66) | | |
| Yes | 69.7% | 65.2% |
| No | 13.6% | 9.1% |
| Difference (Yes/No) | 56.1% | 56.1% |
| No Opinion | 16.7% | 25.8% |
| Clergy (34) | | |
| Yes | 54.1% | 46.0% |
| No | 0.0% | 2.7% |
| Difference (Yes/No) | 54.1% | 43.3% |
| No Opinion | 45.9% | 51.4% |
| Medical Doctors (9) | | |
| Yes | 55.6% | 55.6% |
| No | 11.1% | 22.2% |
| Difference (Yes/No) | 44.5% | 33.4% |
| No Opinion | 33.2% | 22.2% |
| Lawyers (17) | | |
| Yes | 58.8% | 58.8% |
| No | 11.8% | 11.8% |
| Difference (Yes/No) | 47.0% | 47.0% |
| No Opinion | 29.4% | 29.4% |
| Social Agency Personnel (79) | | |
| Yes | 65.3% | 78.7% |
| No | 4.0% | 2.7% |
| Difference (Yes/No) | 61.3% | 76.0% |
| No Opinion | 30.7% | 18.7% |

TABLE 8   Reaction to Proposed Residential Treatment
for Adolescents by Strata

| | Alcohol and Drug Problems | | Emotional Problems | |
| --- | --- | --- | --- | --- |
| | Key Informant | General Public | Key Informant | General Public |
| **Stratum No. 1** | | | | |
| Yes | 63.6% | 69.2% | 57.6% | 75.5% |
| No | 6.1% | 18.1% | 9.1% | 9.6% |
| Difference (Yes/No) | 57.5% | 51.1% | 48.5% | 65.9% |
| No Opinion | 30.3% | 12.8% | 33.3% | 14.9% |
| **Stratum No. 2** | | | | |
| Yes | 65.7% | 75.3% | 70.4% | 74.5% |
| No | 7.6% | 16.0% | 5.2% | 14.5% |
| Difference (Yes/No) | 58.1% | 49.3% | 65.2% | 60.0% |
| No Opinion | 26.7% | 8.2% | 24.4% | 10.1% |
| **Stratum No. 3** | | | | |
| Yes | 63.2% | 71.7% | 66.0% | 73.2% |
| No | 6.3% | 15.1% | 6.3% | 14.5% |
| Difference (No/Yes) | 56.9% | 56.6% | 59.7% | 58.7% |
| No Opinion | 30.6% | 13.3% | 27.8% | 12.4% |
| **Stratum No. 4** | | | | |
| Yes | 60.6% | 67.9% | 64.8% | 59.5% |
| No | 12.7% | 22.6% | 16.9% | 25.0% |
| Difference (Yes/No) | 46.9% | 45.3% | 47.9% | 34.5% |
| No Opinion | 26.8% | 9.5% | 18.3% | 15.5% |
| **Stratum No. 5 (Rural)** | | | | |
| Yes | | 57.1% | | 42.9% |
| No | | 4.8% | | 6.0% |
| Difference (Yes/No) | | 52.3% | | 36.9% |
| No Opinion | | 38.1% | | 51.2% |

# ABOUT THE AUTHORS

Keith A. Neuber, M. S., is currently employed as special services coordinator at the Mental Health Clinic, Quad-City Center, Madison County, Inc., in Granite City, Illinois. Mr. Neuber served as project director for the Mental Health Clinic needs assessment efforts. He received his master's degree in clinical psychology from Eastern Kentucky University in 1975.

William T. Atkins, M.S.W., is the executive director of the Mental Health Clinic, Quad-City Center, Madison County, Inc., in Granite City, Illinois. He is an adjunct instructor at the Delinquency Study and Youth Development Center of Southern Illinois University at Edwardsville, Illinois. Mr. Atkins received his master's degree from St. Louis University, School of Social Work, in 1971.

James A. Jacobson, Ph.D., is an associate professor at the Delinquency Study and Youth Development Center of Southern Illinois University at Edwardsville, Illinois. In addition to research and public service activities, Dr. Jacobson is engaged in teaching in the Human Services Program of the Delinquency Study Center. He received his doctoral degree from St. Louis University in counselor education.

Nicholas A. Reuterman, Ph.D., is director of the Delinquency Study and Youth Development Center of Southern Illinois University at Edwardsville, Illinois. He holds the rank of professor in the Delinquency Study Center and in the Department of Psychology at Southern Illinois University. Dr. Reuterman received his doctoral degree from the University of Colorado in social psychology and has done postdoctoral work at the University of Colorado and the University of Michigan.